GAYLORD F

KINGS & QUEENS

RULERS & DESPOTS

Series Editor:
David Salariya was born in Dundee, Scotland, where he studied illustration and printmaking, concentrating on book design in his post-graduate year. He later completed a further post-graduate course in art education at Sussex University. He has illustrated a wide range of books on botanical, historical, and mythical subjects. He has designed and created many new series of children's books for publishers in the U.K. and United States. In 1989 he established his own publishing company, The Salariya Book Company Ltd. He lives in England with his wife, the illustrator Shirley Willis.

Author:
Fiona Macdonald studied history at Cambridge University and at the University of East Anglia, where she is a part-time tutor. She has written many books for children on historical topics, including *Cities* in the *Timelines* series, and *How Would You Survive as an Aztec?*

Consultant:
Penelope Stewart has a particular interest in royal costume and ceremonies. She has written and contributed to numerous history books for children.

Series Editor	David Salariya
Editor	Jenny Millington
Consultant	Penelope Stewart
Artists	Corinne Burrows
	Ray Burrows
	Simon Calder
	Virginia Gray
	John James
	Syd Lewis
	Mark Peppé
	Lee Peters
	Gerald Wood
Design Assistant	Kate Buxton

Artists
Ray and Corinne Burrows pp 20-21; **Simon Calder** pp 18-19; **Virginia Gray** pp 40-41; **John James** pp 24-25, 28-29, 38-39; **Syd Lewis** pp 22-23, 34-35; **Mark Peppé** pp 6-7, 10-11, 36-37; **Lee Peters** pp 16-17; **Gerald Wood** pp 8-9, 12-13, 14-15, 26-27, 30-31, 32-33.

First published in 1995
by Franklin Watts Books

Franklin Watts
95 Madison Avenue
New York, NY 10016

© The Salariya Book Company Ltd
MCMXCV

Printed in Belgium

Macdonald, Fiona.
   Kings and queens : rulers and despots / by Fiona Macdonald.
     p. cm. — (Timelines)
   Includes index.
   ISBN 0-531-14369-4 (lib. bdg.) — ISBN 0-531-15281-2 (pbk).
   1. World history—Juvenile literature. 2. Kings and rulers—Juvenile literature. 3. Queens—Juvenile literature. 4. Heads of state—Juvenile literature. I. Title. II. Series: Timelines (Franklin Watts, inc.)
D21.3.M27 1995
909.82—dc20
                          95-21702
                          CIP AC

TIMELINES
KINGS &
QUEENS

RULERS & DESPOTS

Written by
FIONA MACDONALD

Created & Designed by
DAVID SALARIYA

FRANKLIN WATTS
A Division of Grolier Publishing
New York•London•Hong Kong•Sydney
Danbury, Connecticut

CONTENTS

6 EARLY RULERS
Strong leaders, the first kings.

8 EGYPT
Pharaohs and queens of Egypt, kings and
leaders of Middle Eastern peoples.

10 ANCIENT GREECE
The rise of city-states, Athens and the
development of democracy.

12 ROME
The the rise of the republic
and the growth of an empire.

14 CELTS, FRANKS, SAXONS, VIKINGS
The end of Roman power and the
rise of the northern peoples.

16 MEDIEVAL ISLAM
The Prophet Muhammad, law and
the Koran, the caliphs.

18 MIDDLE AGES
New rulers in Europe, Muslims in
Spain.

20 MEDIEVAL RULERS
European kings and queens,
conflicts between states.

22 THE FAR EAST
Empires and rulers in China and
Japan.

24 EARLY AMERICA
Central and South American
societies, Native American nations

26 GREAT EMPIRES
The Ottomans and Moguls,
kingdoms of Benin and Zimbabwe.

28 RENAISSANCE EUROPE
Rulers as patrons of the arts, religious problems facing heads of state.

30 ANCIEN RÉGIME
The might of Louis XIV, the French Revolution, the Hapsburg Empire.

32 AMERICA
The American Revolution and independence from Britain.

34 EUROPEAN EMPIRES
The rise and fall of European empires.

36 POWER FOR THE PEOPLE
Kings and queens lose power to the politicians and the people.

38 GREAT DICTATORS
The rise of Fascism and Nazism.

40 POST-WAR WORLD
The formation of the U.N.

42 PAST AND FUTURE
Has monarchy a future? the power of the media – good or bad?

44 TIMELINE

46 GLOSSARY

48 INDEX

EARLY RULERS

△ EVIDENCE of early civilizations has been found in many countries of the world.

△ MEN were respected for their bravery and their physical strength. War leaders had to be young and fit, ready to defend their tribe.

▽ WOMEN were valued for their "magical" ability to give birth to babies who would grow up to continue the tribe. Older women, with wisdom and long experience, might become respected advice-givers.

◁ STONE STATUETTE of a powerful, pregnant woman made in northern Europe around 25,000 B.C. It portrays a fertility goddess, or perhaps a tribal elder. It may have been made as a good luck charm.

▷ IN THE EARLIEST societies, men who were skilled at tracking and chasing game became leaders of the hunt. This was a position of great responsibility and power. The whole tribe depended on the hunt's success.

WHAT MAKES a good king or queen? Over the centuries, a good ruler has been expected to have all kinds of qualities: health, strength, wealth, bravery, wisdom, political cunning, religious faith, royal blood, the ability to produce children – and, if possible, good looks and dignity, as well. Few past rulers had them all; but we still expect our kings, queens, presidents, and prime ministers to possess many of these characteristics.

The earliest rulers were probably leaders of small groups of migratory hunters and gatherers, who lived from around 350,000 years ago. They would have been respected for their physical strength, and for their hunting and survival skills. Men and women leaders may also have played important religious roles, such as magicians, healers, and priests. Nobody knows the names of the first king and queen, but you can find out about some of the earliest known rulers in these pages.

From around 10,000 B.C., human societies began to change. Men and women began to live in settled farming villages, and, from about 6000 B.C., in small market towns. Life became much more organized.

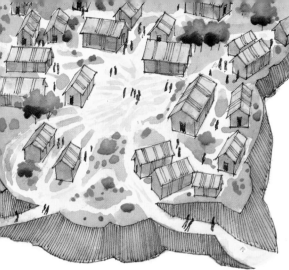

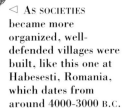

◁ AS SOCIETIES became more organized, well-defended villages were built, like this one at Habesesti, Romania, which dates from around 4000-3000 B.C.

▷ CARVED boundary stone, put up by King Evil-Merodach, who ruled the city-state of Babylon from 721-710 B.C. The king is receiving advice from a god.

Community leaders were now responsible for organizing crop planting and animal grazing, for arranging fresh water supplies, and maintaining strong defences. They had to uphold systems of inheritance, standardize weights and measures, and try to encourage fair trade.

Prince Gilgamesh

△ SCENE reconstructed from the royal standard of Ur, a city in Sumeria (now southern Iraq).

▽ CAVE PAINTING from the Sahara Desert in Africa, showing people herding cattle, 4000-3000 B.C.

▽ MANY STORIES were told about the adventures of an ancient Mesopotamian hero, Prince Gilgamesh. He was ruler of the city of Uruk in Sumeria, sometime between 3000 and 2000 B.C. Gilgamesh was a mighty hunter, "two-thirds god, one-third man." He was strong, wise, and often very cruel.

▷ THE KINGS OF UR and Sumer were originally war leaders, with the title of "lugal," or "great man." It was their duty to command troops in battle.

▷ THE QUEEN OF ASSYRIA feasting. She is seated on a high throne, and surrounded by courtiers and servants. This stone carving was made around 650 B.C.

◁ △ THE ROYAL TOMBS of Ur date from around 2500 B.C. Kings and members of the royal family were buried there, along with weapons, horses, chariots, and rich jewelry made of gold, silver, and lapis lazuli.

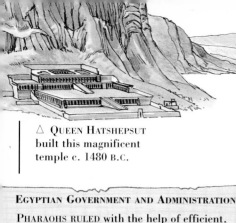

△ QUEEN HATSHEPSUT built this magnificent temple c. 1480 B.C.

EGYPTIAN GOVERNMENT AND ADMINISTRATION

PHARAOHS RULED with the help of efficient, well-trained officials, who were responsible for many different tasks. Officials were recruited from wealthy noble families.

Pharaoh and queen

High priestess

High priest

Grand viziers of Upper and Lower Egypt

Craftsmen

Governors

Scribes

Artists

Tax gatherers

Priests and priestesses

Builders

Farmers

Scribes

Traders

Slaves

△ THE EARLIEST PHARAOHS had been war leaders, who rode into battle on horse-drawn chariots.

EGYPT

IN THE FAR DISTANT PAST, the land of Egypt was two separate kingdoms: Upper Egypt (the south) and Lower Egypt (the Nile delta lands). Around 3100 B.C., Pharaoh Menes united them into one vast new kingdom. The system of government he set up lasted for almost 3000 years. As rulers of Egypt, the pharaohs had many responsibilities: deciding government policy; supervising officials; maintaining law and order; making alliances and sometimes leading armies to war.

But an Egyptian pharaoh was more than just a king. He was the representative of the gods on earth and every day he spoke to them in their temples.

△ TO KEEP the royal family special, pharaohs often chose wives from among their relatives.

◁ QUEEN NEFERTARI (who lived around 1270 B.C.) offering vases of incense to the goddess Hathor.

△ ENEMIES captured in war were brought before the pharaoh, who decided their fate in a special court.

△ PHARAOH RAMSES II ruled 1290-1224 B.C. He built many splendid temples and statues.

△ QUEEN NEFERTITI, wife of Pharaoh Akenaton, as she looked c. 1362 B.C.

△ PHARAOH Tutankhamen's splendid tomb lay hidden until A.D. 1922.

△ QUEEN HATSHEPSUT (ruled c. 1489-1469 B.C.) was one of the few women to govern Egypt.

△ PHARAOH AKENATON (1370-1353 B.C.) founded a religion and built a great new city.

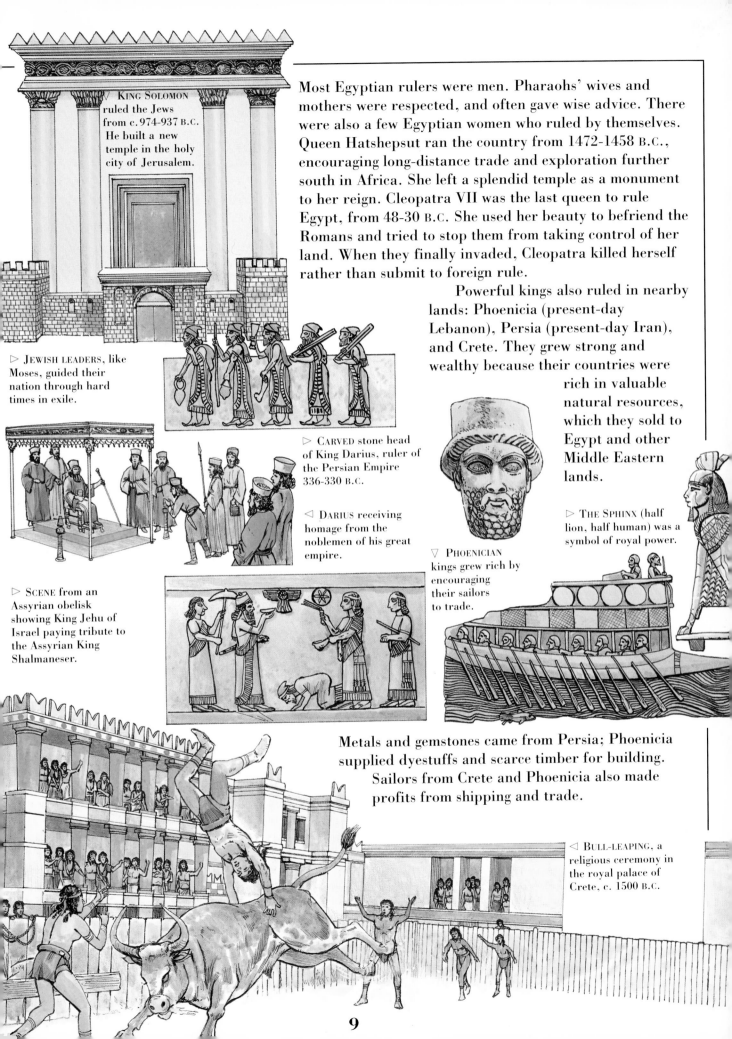

KING SOLOMON ruled the Jews from c. 974-937 B.C. He built a new temple in the holy city of Jerusalem.

Most Egyptian rulers were men. Pharaohs' wives and mothers were respected, and often gave wise advice. There were also a few Egyptian women who ruled by themselves. Queen Hatshepsut ran the country from 1472-1458 B.C., encouraging long-distance trade and exploration further south in Africa. She left a splendid temple as a monument to her reign. Cleopatra VII was the last queen to rule Egypt, from 48-30 B.C. She used her beauty to befriend the Romans and tried to stop them from taking control of her land. When they finally invaded, Cleopatra killed herself rather than submit to foreign rule.

Powerful kings also ruled in nearby lands: Phoenicia (present-day Lebanon), Persia (present-day Iran), and Crete. They grew strong and wealthy because their countries were rich in valuable natural resources, which they sold to Egypt and other Middle Eastern lands.

▷ JEWISH LEADERS, like Moses, guided their nation through hard times in exile.

▷ CARVED stone head of King Darius, ruler of the Persian Empire 336-330 B.C.

◁ DARIUS receiving homage from the noblemen of his great empire.

▷ THE SPHINX (half lion, half human) was a symbol of royal power.

▽ PHOENICIAN kings grew rich by encouraging their sailors to trade.

▷ SCENE from an Assyrian obelisk showing King Jehu of Israel paying tribute to the Assyrian King Shalmaneser.

Metals and gemstones came from Persia; Phoenicia supplied dyestuffs and scarce timber for building. Sailors from Crete and Phoenicia also made profits from shipping and trade.

◁ BULL-LEAPING, a religious ceremony in the royal palace of Crete, c. 1500 B.C.

9

ANCIENT GREECE

△ GREEK CITY-STATES were founded in western Turkey as well as on the Greek mainland and islands.

△ ONE OF THE EARLIEST and most famous works of Greek literature, the *Iliad*, tells the story of the war between Greece and Troy (in Turkey), and describes the brave and sometimes foolish actions of leaders on both sides: Hector, Achilles, Priam, Paris, Menelaus, and Agamemnon.

◁ GOLD BURIAL MASK, c. 1500 B.C., excavated from a royal grave at the Greek city-state of Mycenae. We do not know which king was buried here.

▽ DECORATED CUP showing King Arkesilas of Cyrene, a Greek colony in North Africa. He is seated (left) on a throne, supervising the weighing and packing of valuable goods. This cup was made in or near Sparta, c. 560 B.C.

THE EARLIEST GREEK RULERS were warrior kings. Together with their noble followers, they colonized small, isolated territories known as city-states. From the rich tombs and massive buildings they left behind, we know that they were rich and powerful. For many centuries (from around 1600 B.C. or earlier, to around 800 B.C.) their task was to defend their city and its citizens from invasion or attack.

Gradually, conditions in Greece became more settled. Trade flourished, laws were written down, and new groups of people – wealthy merchants and members of the citizen army – began to seek power. New kinds of rulers, called tyrants, replaced old-style kings and made many new laws.

▷ UNTIL AROUND 750 B.C., most city-states were ruled by kings or by wealthy nobles, who rode to war on fine horses.

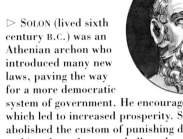

Solon

△ WHEN ATHENS first began to grow into a city, it was ruled by "archons" (officials) elected by wealthy men. They made stern laws to govern trade. Draco, who was an archon in 621 B.C., was the first person to write these laws down.

▷ SOLON (lived sixth century B.C.) was an Athenian archon who introduced many new laws, paving the way for a more democratic system of government. He encouraged trade, which led to increased prosperity. Solon abolished the custom of punishing debtors by making them slaves, and allowed wealthy foreign merchants to become citizens of Athens. He got rid of many of Draco's strict laws and harsh punishments.

△ TYRANTS were often unpopular rulers. This urn depicts a tyrant being assassinated.

▽ THE BOULEUTERION (council chamber) in Athens, where the 500 members of the Boulé (council) met.

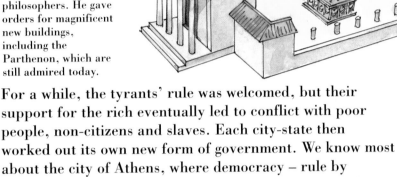

▷ PERICLES (lived c. 495-429 B.C.), soldier and statesman. He led Athens during its greatest period of democracy, and was a friend of leading writers and philosophers. He gave orders for magnificent new buildings, including the Parthenon, which are still admired today.

▽ ALL ADULT MALE citizens living in democratic city-states had the right to attend the assembly, which met once a week to discuss new ideas and vote on future policies. Famous orators, like Demosthenes (lived 384-322 B.C.), learned how to influence the mood of the Assembly with their passionate speeches.

For a while, the tyrants' rule was welcomed, but their support for the rich eventually led to conflict with poor people, non-citizens and slaves. Each city-state then worked out its own new form of government. We know most about the city of Athens, where democracy – rule by citizens – was introduced by reformer Cleisthenes in 508-507 B.C. From then on, all adult male citizens had the right to share in government.

Things were very different in Athens' rival city, Sparta. There, two kings and a council of elders ruled over an elite group of citizens – organized rather like an army – and a large number of helots (semi-slaves).

▽ ALEXANDER the Great (ruled 336-323 B.C.), king of the small northern Greek state of Macedon, aimed to be ruler of the whole world. From 334-323 B.C., he led his army to conquests from Egypt and Persia to the Himalayas.

△ COIN showing the head of Alexander the Great, minted c. 300 B.C. Alexander's conquest of the mighty Persian Empire meant gold and silver became more abundant in Greece.

11

ROME

△ ROMULUS AND REMUS, legendary founders of Rome. Stories told how they were abandoned as babies, then found and brought up by a wolf.

ACCORDING to ancient tradition, the city of Rome was founded in 753 B.C. It was ruled by kings. Romulus was the first; Tarquin the Proud was the seventh and last. In 509 B.C. he was expelled by the citizens for his cruelty. A new form of government, called a republic, was established.

The republic was designed to stop a single ruler from ever growing powerful again. Rome was governed by two Consuls, elected each year, and advised by the Senate – a group of experienced former officials. Consuls, senators, and junior officials came from the patrician (noble) class.

By 31 B.C., Rome had grown rich and very powerful. It ruled over a large empire in Europe and the Middle East. Republican government had worked well while Rome was still a small city, but was not so suitable for ruling an empire. There were quarrels among rival senators. Army commanders such as Julius Caesar began to seek political power. Caesar was murdered in 44 B.C., but this did not solve Rome's political problems.

△ TARQUIN was the last king of Rome. He was proud and cruel.

△ HE KILLED rich men to get their land, and took away civil rights.

△ HE LED the Roman army to victory against neighboring peoples.

△ BUT AFTER RULING for 24 years, he was deposed and exiled.

△ THE LAND surrounding the city of Rome belonged to the Etruscans. Their most famous leader Lars Porsena, led many attacks on Rome.

△ ARMY GENERAL and bodyguard, from a tomb made in the second century A.D. (Left) A soldier from the elite Praetorian Guard.

◁ CENSORS were important government officials. They kept records of all the citizens who held property in Rome. Aediles were officials responsible for public works, such as the city's water supply.

◁ JULIUS CAESAR (100-44 B.C.). He began his career as a soldier, but had ambitions to be sole ruler of Rome. He was assassinated after declaring himself "dictator for life."

◁ MARCUS Tullius Cicero (106-43 B.C.) was a top politician, and public speaker.

▷ POMPEY the Great (lived 106-48 B.C.). He was a brilliant army commander.

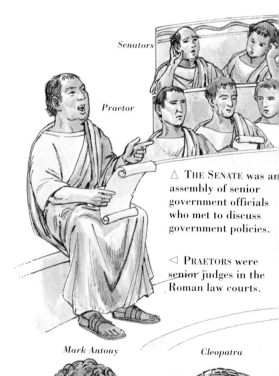

Senators

Praetor

△ THE SENATE was an assembly of senior government officials who met to discuss government policies.

◁ PRAETORS were senior judges in the Roman law courts.

Mark Antony

Cleopatra

△ MARK ANTONY (c. 83-30 B.C.) seized power after the death of Julius Caesar. He fell in love with Queen Cleopatra VII of Egypt (69-30 B.C.). They fought Rome, but were defeated and killed themsel

△ LANDS belonging to the Roman Empire at the height of Roman power, around A.D. 112.

△ AUGUSTUS, the first Roman emperor, who ruled from 27 B.C. to A.D. 14.

△ EMPEROR TIBERIUS ruled A.D. 14-37. His reign was disastrous. He probably killed his own son and heir, Germanicus, and he employed a brutal soldier, Sejanus, as his chief advisor and helper.

△ EMPEROR NERO ruled from A.D. 54-68. At first he listened to wise advisors, but later spent all his time singing, acting, and chariot racing. He cruelly persecuted the Christians. He was deposed in A.D. 68, and forced to kill himself.

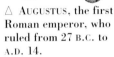

◁▷ TWO CONSULS were elected each year from among the senators.

△ EMPEROR TRAJAN ruled A.D. 98-117. He was a popular and successful army leader, and won many new lands for Rome. He made the empire rich and planned many big new building projects, including a new Forum.

△ EMPEROR HADRIAN ruled from A.D. 117-138. Born in Spain, he was unpopular in Rome. He spent most of his reign touring the frontier provinces. In Britain, he organized the building of a long defensive wall between England and Scotland.

△ DEAD EMPERORS who had ruled well were proclaimed gods. This ivory plaque (fourth century A.D.) shows an "apotheosis" – an emperor who has become a god is carried up to heaven.

△ EMPEROR DIOCLETIAN ruled A.D. 284-305. He began his career as an ordinary soldier, and rose through the ranks because of his skill. In A.D. 286, he reorganized the empire's entire administration.

△ EMPEROR CONSTANTINE ruled A.D. 306-337, although he only won control of the empire in A.D. 324. He encouraged Christianity, and moved the empire's capital from Rome to Constantinople.

▷ TEMPLES were dedicated to the spirits of dead emperors. This is the temple of Emperor Claudius in Colchester, in eastern England.

In 43 B.C. Caesar's nephew, Octavian, forced the Senate to make him Consul. In 31 B.C. he declared himself "first citizen" of Rome. He had become, in effect, a king. In 27 B.C. he became emperor, with the name "Augustus."

▷ CELTS, FRANKS, Saxons, and Vikings all lived in northern Europe. The lands they ruled changed over time. At first the Celts occupied most of Europe, except for the far north. By A.D. 900, they had been driven into western lands by Franks, Saxons, and Vikings.

Map labels: Norway, Sweden, Scotland, Denmark, Iceland, England, Poland, Belgium, Germany, France, Caspian Sea, Italy, Spain, Africa, Mediterranean Sea

CELTS, FRANKS, SAXONS, VIKINGS

FROM AROUND 800 B.C. to around A.D. 1000, the peoples of northern Europe competed with each other and the Roman Empire for land. They were led by warrior kings (and a few famous queens), honored for their bravery in battle. It was the kings' duty to uphold ancient tribal traditions, to provide justice, to reward loyal warriors with rich gifts, to be generous hosts and good companions, to act as patrons of poets and craft workers and, after around A.D. 600, to protect the Christian church.

▷ EACH Celtic tribe had its own king or queen. In disputes between tribes, the ruler of a small tribe would sometimes buy the help of a larger, more powerful one with gifts or hostages.

▷ THE CELTS often wore brightly colored clothes of wool woven in checked patterns. Men wore trousers under a tunic. Men and women both wore cloaks fastened at the neck with a brooch.

▽ CELTIC LEADERS were expected to be bold and brave in battle.

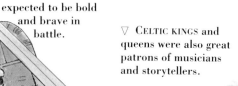

▽ CELTIC KINGS and queens were also great patrons of musicians and storytellers.

△ VERCINGETORIX was a Celtic chief who lived in France. He was a brave fighter and a good commander. He led a huge army against Julius Caesar and the Roman army in 52 B.C. He was captured by the Romans, imprisoned, then put to death.

△ AMBIORIX was a Celtic chief who lived in Belgium. He fought against Julius Caesar and the Roman army in A.D. 54. Although all his lands were occupied, Ambiorix was never captured, but had to spend the rest of his life on the run.

△ BOUDICCA was queen of the Iceni, a Celtic tribe who lived in southeast England. After Boudicca's husband died in A.D. 60, the Romans refused to let her rule, so she rebelled. Her army was defeated by the Romans.

△ COIN showing Attila the Hun, leader of a nomad people from Central Asia who invaded Europe in the fifth century A.D.

▷ THEODORIC, king of the Ostrogoths, a nomadic people from eastern Europe, from A.D. 471-526. He invaded Italy in A.D. 489, and set up a new kingdom there. He ruled wisely and well.

When Roman power faded, in the fifth century A.D., Germanic peoples – the Franks, Angles, and Saxons – became rulers in north-west Europe. In the sixth century A.D., new groups of invaders arrived from Central Asia.

The first migrants were the Celts, who set out around 800 B.C. from their homeland in the Alps. By 200 B.C., they had established kingdoms in north Italy, Britain, and France. At the same time, Slav peoples colonized Poland, Russia, and the Ukraine. From around 100 B.C., Celts and Slavs all had to fight against Rome.

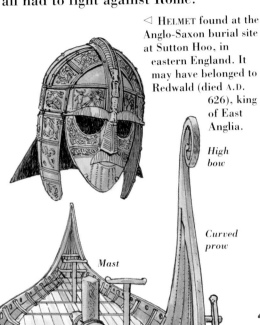

◁ HELMET found at the Anglo-Saxon burial site at Sutton Hoo, in eastern England. It may have belonged to Redwald (died A.D. 626), king of East Anglia.

High bow

Curved prow

Mast

Steering oar

▷ VIKING KINGS and jarls ordered fine new warships to be built for themselves and their warrior bands. They gave them names like "Wave Rider" or "Sea Serpent."

△ KING CHARLEMAGNE of the Franks (ruled A.D. 771-814) was one of the most powerful French kings.

△ KING EDWARD the Confessor (ruled 1042-1066) was the last Anglo-Saxon king of England.

▷ VIKING KINGS and queens often paid to build churches in newly settled lands. This church was built in Iceland around A.D. 1000.

△ KING ALFRED the Great ruled Wessex from A.D. 871-899. He led Anglo-Saxon armies against Viking invaders from Denmark. He founded many new towns and was a great patron of religion and learning.

▷ VIKING kingship was based on success in war.

In Scandinavia, by around A.D. 800, the first Viking warrior kings were beginning to rise to power. But the boundaries between all these migrant peoples remained uncertain for many years, so they were often at war.

◁ PAGAN Saxon and Viking rulers were often buried in boat-shaped graves. Sometimes a real boat was used. It was set on fire, so the flames could carry the dead king's soul to the next world.

MEDIEVAL ISLAM

The Angel Gabriel, from a fifteenth-century Persian manuscript.

◁ THE PROPHET MUHAMMAD (c 570-632) received the text of the holy book called the Koran in a series of revelations from God. The first revelation was announced by the Angel Gabriel. God's words in the Koran became the basis of the religion of Islam.

△ CALIPHS were rulers of Muslim people. They had to: (1) Run the government.

(2) Act as chief judge in the courts. All Muslim laws were based on the Koran.

(3) As "Commander of the Faithful," each caliph was in charge of the army.

(4) Lead public prayers and sometimes preach in the mosque.

△ AFTER the fourth caliph, Ali (ruled 656-661), was murdered, his supporters, called Shi'ites, broke away from other Muslims, and followed their own religious leaders instead of the caliphs.

THE PROPHET MUHAMMAD died in A.D. 632, but his life influenced Muslim rulers for centuries. Muhammad had preached God's message, which he had received in a series of revelations. After his death, this message was written down in a book known as the Koran. Muslims believe that the Koran teaches everyone – from kings and queens to ordinary people – the right way to live. Muslim law – called Shariyah (the straight path) – was also based on the Koran. It covered all aspects of life, from buying and selling goods to saying prayers. It was every Muslim ruler's duty to uphold Shariyah. Any new laws they made were also meant to follow the teachings of the Koran.

While Muhammad was alive, the first Muslims had relied on him. After his death they chose Abu Bakr (ruled 632-634), his friend and advisor to lead them.

△ THE GREAT MOSQUE at Damascus, built by the fifth caliph, Mu'awiya (ruled 661-680), and his descendants. (Below) The caliph's bath-house in Baghdad, in the eighth century A.D.

▽ IN 762, the caliphs made Baghdad (in present-day Iraq) their capital. It grew very quickly. By 814 it was the world's biggest city.

They gave Abu Bakr the title of "Caliph" (successor), and he ruled wisely and well. As caliph, he had authority over the entire Muslim world, although he relied on local princes, government officials, and army commanders to help him rule.

Coin showing Caliph al-Mutawakkil,

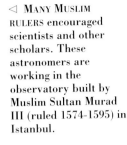

◁ MANY MUSLIM RULERS encouraged scientists and other scholars. These astronomers are working in the observatory built by Muslim Sultan Murad III (ruled 1574-1595) in Istanbul.

Abu Bakr and the three caliphs who ruled after him (Umar 634-644, Uthman 644-656, and Ali 656-651) are known as the "rightly-guided" caliphs, because they all knew Muhammad, and had his example to follow.

▷ MINARET (tower used to call Muslims to prayer five times a day) of the Great Mosque at Samarra, in Iraq. The caliphs built a palace-city here to escape from the noise and dangers of Baghdad.

◁ CALIPH Al-Hakim ruled during the eleventh century. He was often mentally ill. He destroyed churches and mistreated his critics – whatever faith they were.

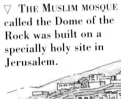

◁ SULTAN Salah al-Din (Saladin) lived from 1137-1193. He was a great war leader who won famous victories against Christian troops during the Crusades.

▽ THE MUSLIM MOSQUE called the Dome of the Rock was built on a specially holy site in Jerusalem.

◁ JERUSALEM was holy to Jews, Christians, and Muslims. For centuries, there were quarrels over who should rule it.

Later caliphs lived very different lives. Some, like Harun al-Rashid (ruled 786-809), were fabulously wealthy and great patrons of art and learning. Others, like Mu'awiya (ruled 661-680), were soldiers and administrators.

◁ MANY MUSLIM LEADERS were buried in magnificent tombs. This is the tomb of Ismail Samanid, ruler of Bukhara, in Central Asia, who died in 907.

▷ SOUTHERN SPAIN was ruled by Muslim princes from 711-1492. They built splendid mosques and palaces, with elaborately decorated windows and doors.

△ SULTAN Alp Arslan, who ruled the Seljuk Turks (nomads who settled in Turkey) from 1063-1072.

MIDDLE AGES

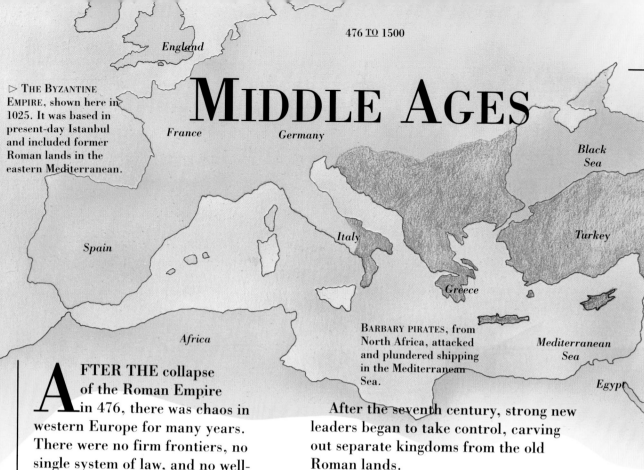

▷ THE BYZANTINE EMPIRE, shown here in 1025. It was based in present-day Istanbul and included former Roman lands in the eastern Mediterranean.

England

France *Germany*

Black Sea

Spain

Italy

Turkey

Greece

Africa

BARBARY PIRATES, from North Africa, attacked and plundered shipping in the Mediterranean Sea.

Mediterranean Sea

Egypt

A FTER THE collapse of the Roman Empire in 476, there was chaos in western Europe for many years. There were no firm frontiers, no single system of law, and no well-trained army to keep the peace. Above all, there were no "ready-made" kings to replace the Roman emperors. Warlords, invaders, and local chieftains all struggled for power.

After the seventh century, strong new leaders began to take control, carving out separate kingdoms from the old Roman lands.

In the eighth century, southern Spain was invaded by Muslim troops from North Africa. They were stopped from marching farther north, and taking control of all Europe, by defeat at the battle of Poitiers in 732.

▷ ROMULUS AUGUSTULUS was the last Roman emperor to rule in western Europe. He was deposed by invaders in 476. Italy was without stable government for over 50 years, until Justinian seized power.

▷ DURING the seventh and eighth centuries A.D., the Byzantine Empire was attacked by pagan Slav peoples from the north, and by Muslim Arab forces from the south and east.

▽ BYZANTINE EMPEROR JUSTINIAN portrayed in a glittering mosaic, surrounded by nobles, bodyguards and priests. This mosaic decorates the church of San Vitale, Ravenna, Italy, which Justinian's troops recaptured from invaders in A.D. 540.

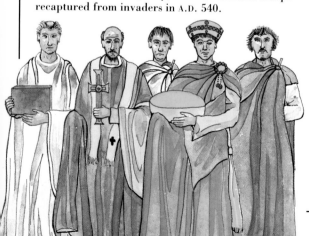

△ DANISH KING Harald Bluetooth (ruled 950-985) was the first Christian king among the Vikings. He also won fame for the great buildings he planned.

△ IN NORTHERN EUROPE, new ruling families came to power. Henry I "the Fowler" ruled Saxony (part of Germany) from 919-936. He founded a dynasty of strong kings.

▽ IN RUSSIA, Vladimir the Great ruled from 978-1015. He was a brave war leader, sponsored art and trade, and encouraged Christianity in Russia.

In eastern Europe, a new dynasty of emperors, known as the Byzantines, led a Roman-style government from the city of Constantinople. The Byzantine Empire was often attacked by rivals in Syria, Iraq, and Iran. There were palace murders, conspiracies, and feuds. Even so, the empire survived until 1453.

Some medieval rulers – like Henry III of Germany (ruled 1039-1046) or Byzantine Emperor Justinian I (ruled 527-565) – were admired for bringing peace. Others, like Jaime I of Aragon (ruled 1213-1276) and Matthias Corvinus of Hungary (ruled 1458-1490) were praised as soldiers, but feared.

▷ IN 1066, Duke William of Normandy (in France) conquered England. He founded a new dynasty – the Normans – and introduced many French words, laws, and ideas about government into England.

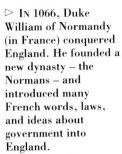

◁ OTTO I "the Great" was king of Germany and Holy Roman Emperor from 936-973. He used the power of the Church to help rule his lands.

▷ KING JOHN ruled England 1199-1216. In 1215 he signed Magna Carta, guaranteeing nobles' rights.

King John signs Magna Carta, 1215.

◁ COUNCILS and parliaments helped kings govern medieval Europe. This is King Edward IV's household council. Its members ran the royal court – and the national government between 1461-1483.

△ THE POPE is head of the Roman Catholic Church. He has spiritual authority, plus lands, laws, and a staff of well-educated priests and scholars. Early popes were often more powerful than kings.

△ BYZANTINE Emperor Constantine VI (ruled 776-797) meets church dignitaries.

◁ KINGS sometimes clashed with church leaders over who had the ultimate power. In 1170, King Henry II of England ordered the murder of Archbishop Thomas à Becket.

▷ KINGS AND QUEENS encouraged art and architecture by commissioning illustrated manuscripts and new building plans. They also rewarded artists and scholars who dedicated their works to them.

Medieval heraldic banners

MEDIEVAL RULERS

▷ BYZANTINE EMPRESS Theodora (ruled 527-547). At first an actress and dancer, she later married Justinian the Great. She was wise, brave, and intelligent, and helped him to rule.

◁ KING ROGER II of Sicily (lived 1105-1154) was a bold battle commander. He was also a great patron of art and learning, and encouraged Jewish, Christian, and Muslim scholars to work together at his court.

▷ BYZANTINE EMPRESS Irene was regent for her son from 780-797. Then she blinded him, and ruled until 802.

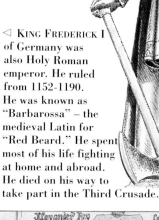

▷ KING ALFRED the Great of Wessex ruled 871-899. He led the Anglo-Saxon defense of England against Viking invaders. He reorganized the army and established the first English navy.

▷ KING LOUIS IX of France (ruled 1226-1270) spent many years abroad, fighting in the Crusades. He was captured and put in prison in Egypt. As soon as he was set free, he went back to fight again. He died of plague, caught during the wars.

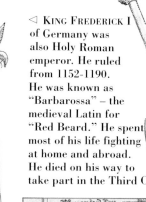

◁ KING FREDERICK I of Germany was also Holy Roman emperor. He ruled from 1152-1190. He was known as "Barbarossa" – the medieval Latin for "Red Beard." He spent most of his life fighting at home and abroad. He died on his way to take part in the Third Crusade.

△ KING EDWARD I of England (ruled 1272-1307), shown here in Parliament with King Alexander III of Scotland and Prince Llewellyn of Wales. Edward was famous as a lawmaker. He fought in the Crusades, and against the Welsh and the Scots.

△ KING LOUIS IX was made a saint in 1297.

△ ALFONSO V (called "the Magnanimous") was king of Aragon (Spain) from 1416-1458.

◁ CHARLES THE BOLD, Duke of Burgundy 1467-1477, shown here with his wife Isabelle. They ruled over a wealthy, artistic and glamorous court.

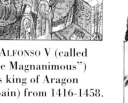

△ CHARLES V "the Wise," king of France 1364-1380. He led French armies to many victories against England.

▽ KING FERDINAND of Aragon and Queen Isabella of Castile, joint rulers of Spain 1479-1504. They financed the voyage of Christopher Columbus to America in 1492.

△ HOLY ROMAN emperor Otto III (ruled 983-1002). He aimed to re-create the power of the old Roman Empire and made the Pope his tutor.

▽ QUEEN MELISENDE (ruled 1126-1160) was queen of the Christian Crusader kingdom of Jerusalem.

△ QUEEN ELEANOR of Aquitaine (lived 1122-1204) married two kings: Louis VII of France and Henry II of England. She had great determination; she was imprisoned for supporting her sons when they rebelled.

◁ WHEN HER HUSBAND, King Louis VIII, died, Blanche of Castile, queen of France, ruled the kingdom from 1226-1234, while her son was a child. She was wise, scholarly, and firm.

◁ ROBERT THE BRUCE, king of Scotland 1306-1329, led the Scots' fight for independence against King Edward I of England.

▷ THE LEOPARDS of England, royal standard of King Richard the Lionheart.

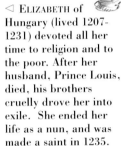

▷ KING RICHARD I "the Lionheart" (ruled 1189-1199) was famous for his skill as a war leader in the Crusades. He became one of England's most popular kings, even though he spent most of his reign abroad, and could not speak English – only Latin and French.

◁ ELIZABETH of Hungary (lived 1207-1231) devoted all her time to religion and to the poor. After her husband, Prince Louis, died, his brothers cruelly drove her into exile. She ended her life as a nun, and was made a saint in 1235.

◁ KING EDWARD III of England (ruled 1327-1377). He began the Hundred Years' War with France. He was famous for his bravery and military skill.

▽ PRINCE DMITRI of Russia won a famous victory against the Tatars in 1380.

△ HENRY V of England (ruled 1413-1422) led his soldiers to victory against the French at the Battle of Agincourt in 1415.

△ HENRY VI of England (ruled 1422-1461 and 1470-1471) was mentally ill. Wise councilors helped him rule.

◁ PRINCE HENRY the Navigator of Portugal (lived 1394-1460) sponsored many voyages by leading explorers.

△ RICHARD III of England (ruled 1483-1485) seized power to become king. Stories told how he murdered his nephews, the "Princes in the Tower," because some people said they had more right to rule. He was killed in a battle against Henry Tudor, a rival for the throne. Later, Henry Tudor became King Henry VII.

◁ CONSTANTINE XI (ruled 1448-1453) was the last Byzantine emperor. He died heroically, defending his country.

THE FAR EAST

FROM EARLIEST TIMES, the problem facing Chinese rulers was how to control their huge kingdom. They did not always succeed, and for over five centuries China was divided into about 100 smaller states that were constantly at war. Then in 221 B.C., Qin Shi Huangdi, the first Chinese emperor, came to power. Under his strong – but brutal – rule, China was united. The emperor controlled the army, collected taxes, and demanded work service from adult men. Strict new laws were passed, making villagers responsible for each other's good behavior. Noble families no longer had the right to rule.

△ THE KING of Hsia, legendary first ruler of China, may in fact have lived around 1500 B.C.

△ SHANG DYNASTY kings (who lived between 1766-1122 B.C.) were buried with their chariots.

▷ THE FIRST DOCUMENTS describing Chinese kings were written by scholars around 1500 B.C.

▷ TERRACOTTA warrior from the tomb of Qin Shi Huangdi, the first Chinese emperor (ruled 221-206 B.C.).

△ QIN SHI HUANGDI'S tomb contained over 1,000 figures.

◁ CHINESE philosopher Confucius (K'ung Fu-tse), lived 551-479 B.C. He taught that rulers should *encourage* good behavior by citizens, rather than punishing them for bad behavior.

▽ LATER Chinese emperors lived in the Forbidden City, a huge palace complex, begun in 1420.

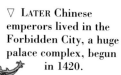

△ THE FIRST Chinese emperor ordered many ambitious building projects. The most famous were the 1500-mile-long Great Wall (begun in 208 B.C.) and a vast network of canals.

△ AFTER a palace plot and a rebellion, Emperor Ming Huang was forced to flee in A.D. 755.

△ EMPEROR Song Taizu encouraged army engineers to use clever new bridge-building techniques.

△ EMPEROR Tang Tai-tsung (ruled 626-649) encouraged useful contacts with other civilizations.

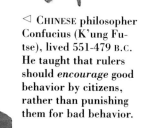

△ EMPEROR Chu Yuan-chang (ruled 1368-1398) was a monk, and then a bandit, before seizing power.

△ EMPEROR Yung-lo (ruled 1402-1424) was a very powerful ruler. He defeated the Mongols and founded a new capital at Beijing.

△ CIXI (Tsu-hsi) (ruled 1862-1908) was the last Chinese empress. After her husband the emperor died, she refused let her son rule.

▽ WARRIOR NOBLES, known as samurai, controlled large areas of Japan from the twelfth to the nineteenth centuries A.D. They fought each other to win extra power. Each samurai leader maintained a private army of well-trained soldiers.

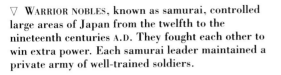

▷ MONGOL LEADER Genghis Khan (ruled 1206-1227) chose his royal name himself. It means "world ruler." His armies conquered lands from northern China to the Black Sea. Genghis was a ruthless soldier and a skillful administrator.

In other eastern lands, many kings and princes won fame as defenders of traditional beliefs. Sometimes they expected divine help. Hindu king Jayavarman of Cambodia (modern Kampuchea) was defeated in battle in 1177. He felt abandoned by the Hindu gods, so he turned to Buddhism instead. He built a whole new palace-city, called Angkor Thom, dedicated to his new-found faith.

The government was run by well-trained officials (called mandarins) recruited by tough examinations from the most intelligent and hardworking men in the land. Noble families no longer had the right to rule. Shi Huangdi's system of government lasted for over 2000 years, until 1911.

In China and Japan, rulers originally had religious as well as political duties. Japanese emperors were said to be descended from the sun goddess. After 1192, shoguns ("barbarian-defeating generals") ran the government. One dynasty of shoguns – the Tokugawa – controlled Japan from 1603-1868. The emperor remained ceremonially important, but was politically feeble. But in 1868 the Meiji emperor dismissed the shogun and reclaimed royal power.

▷ SAMURAI and their families ruled the peasants living on the land surrounding their castles.

▷ TIMUR, or "Tamerlane" (ruled 1369-1405), was Mongol king of Samarkand, in Central Asia. He spent his life conquering new lands, from the Middle East to the borders of China.

◁ MONGOL SOLDIERS were very skillful riders. They rode small, agile ponies, and used them to make hit-and-run raids. They could also turn around in the saddle and fire back at the enemy as their horses carried them away to safety.

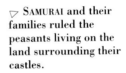

▷ SAMURAI built large castles, like this early seventeenth-century one at Himeji.

▽ FIFTEENTH-CENTURY kings of the Khmer people built temple-palace cities, like Angkor Wat in present-day Kampuchea (Cambodia).

EARLY AMERICA

THE MAYA, AZTEC, AND INCA rulers of Central and South America ruled over rich empires and many conquered peoples. Most South American rulers were war leaders. But they had ceremonial duties, too. They had to say prayers and make sacrifices of enemy captives or their own blood. The Aztecs, especially, feared that if ceremonies were not performed correctly and at the right times, the world would come to an end. In 1502 Aztec leader Tlatoani Montezuma II had 5000 prisoners of war at his coronation to bring blessings on his reign.

Native American nations

Aztecs

Incas

Maya

△ THE AMERICAN continent was home to many different Native peoples, with their own civilizations.

▷ INSIDE a tlatoani's (Aztec ruler's) palace. He and his sons are seated on a raised platform. Everyone else sits on the ground.

△ AZTEC tlatoani rewarded soldiers who served them well with gifts of uniforms, weapons, and jewels. They might even make them nobles.

◁ AZTEC PEOPLES' lives were governed by strict rules, made by the tlatoani, about work, food, good behavior and even the clothes they were allowed to wear. Only rich men (far left) could wear bright, patterned cloaks. Poor men (left) had to wear plain clothing.

▽ SOLID GOLD jewelry from Aztec lands. Only Aztec rulers could afford jewels like this.

Pectoral

Ring

Lip plug

THE MAYA

△ ITZCOATL (left, ruled 1428-1436) allied Aztecs with neighboring cities to form a great empire.

▷ MAYAN RULER Shield Jaguar watches while his wife Lady Xoc makes an offering of blood to the gods in 709.

△ INCA GOVERNMENT officials kept records of tribute payments on knotted strings, called qipus.

▷ MONTEZUMA II (ruled 1502-1520) was the last Aztec tlatoani to rule before the Spanish conquerors arrived.

◁ HERNAN CORTÉS, the Spanish explorer, first met Montezuma II in 1519. By 1521, he had destroyed the Aztec capital city of Tenochtitlan.

▽ THE ROYAL PALACE in the Inca city of Machu Picchu, on a spectacular site high up in the Andes mountains. It was built soon after 1200 by peasants forced to work for the royal family.

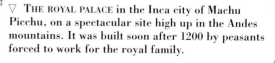

Mayan temple

In North America, there were many Native nations (between 200 and 300 in 1600), living in different environments and following different lifestyles. They governed themselves in different ways, as well. In the southwest, members of pueblos (villages) made collective decisions. In the northwest, large family groups were governed by wealthy elders. On the Great Plains, chiefs (senior warriors and hunters) met in councils to discuss future plans.

▷ SATANTA (lived 1830-1878) was a chief of the Kiowa nation. He was famous as a public speaker. He was put in prison by the U.S. government, and died there.

▷ CHIEF JOSEPH (died 1904) was a leader of the Nez Percé nation. He argued for peace, because wars brought so much suffering to his people.

▷ MESA VERDE, Colorado. About 400 people lived in this pueblo in 1250. It was abandoned around 1400. Pueblos had no special rulers. Men gathered in underground meeting rooms, called kivas, to discuss how the pueblo should be run.

◁ USUALLY, women could not attend Native American council meetings. But they could stand nearby and shout to make their opinions known.

▽ NATIVE AMERICAN nations held councils to make plans and enforce rules for good behavior. All well-respected men might be members. All council members could speak, and were listened to without interruption.

▷ SITTING BULL (lived c. 1834-1890) was a chief of the Sioux Nation. He led them against the U.S. army, and won a famous victory at the Battle of Little Bighorn, 1876.

▷ GERONIMO (also called Goyathlay) lived 1829-1909. He was a brave and fierce chief of the Apache Nation. He fought to save his people from being moved to reservations.

▷ TOTEM POLES – tall, carved, painted tree trunks, decorated with magical designs – recorded a leader's achievements, and the great deeds of his ancestors.

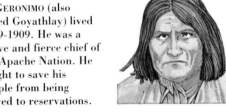

Unlike South America, there were no kings among the North American peoples. But during the nineteenth century, when Native American lands were threatened by European settlers, brave and determined chiefs led the fight to preserve the native homelands and traditional ways of life.

△ IN THE LATE sixteenth century, five small Iroquois nations from the northeast joined together in the Iroquois League. They held council meetings to discuss how the League should be run.

◁ OTTOMAN Sultan Bajazet I (ruled 1389-1402) seated on a high throne, surrounded by courtiers and advisors.

Black Sea

Italy

Mediterranean Sea

Africa

◁ THE OTTOMAN EMPIRE lasted until 1922, but gradually grew weaker.

Arab

Red Sea

△ THE OTTOMAN EMPIRE at its most powerful, late sixteenth century.

GREAT EMPIRES

IN 1258, MONGOL SOLDIERS destroyed Baghdad, city of the caliphs. It was a great blow to Muslim power and prestige. But soon, a new Muslim state based in Turkey began to flourish. It was ruled by the Ottoman dynasty (family), which took its name from its founder, a soldier named Uthman, who ruled from 1281-1324. The sultans (princes) who succeeded him set out to conquer new lands. By 1402, the Ottoman Empire stretched from Serbia to Syria. In 1453, led by Sultan Mehmet II (ruled 1451-1481), the Ottomans conquered the Byzantine capital, Constantinople.

◁ SULTAN Suleyman the Magnificent (ruled 1520-1566). His armies conquered many lands. He was a great patron of art and architecture. He built some of the world's most beautiful mosques.

▷ SULEYMAN the Magnificent's tomb, close to the mosque he paid for in Constantinople (now Istanbul).

△ SULEYMAN also reformed many Ottoman laws. He was known as "the law-giver."

△ SULEYMAN'S favorite wife, Roxelana, was intelligent and beautiful.

△ SULTAN MEHMET II "the Conqueror" (ruled 1451-1481). In 1453 he captured the city of Constantinople and re-named it Istanbul.

Sultan Suleyman the Magnificent ruled from 1520-1566. During his reign the Ottoman Empire expanded further, to North Africa, Arabia, Iran, Bosnia, and Hungary. By 1566, it covered a million square miles.

In India the Muslim Mogul dynasty, founded by a Central Asian prince named Babur (ruled 1526-1530), also achieved success. Like the Ottomans, the Mogul style of government mixed traditional Muslim values with policies suited to local conditions.

Pakistan

India

▽ BABUR, the first Mogul emperor (ruled 1526-1530). His descendants ruled India for 300 years.

Sri Lanka

▷ OTTOMAN and Spanish fleets fought the battle of Lepanto in 1571 for control of the Mediterranean. The Spanish won.

△ HAMIDA, wife of Mogul Emperor Humayun (ruled 1530-1556). She made a heroic escape across the desert while pregnant.

△ EMPEROR Jehangir (ruled 1605-1627). With his wife, Nur Jehan, he encouraged peace and prosperity.

△ AKBAR (ruled 1556-1605) was the greatest Mogul emperor. He fought to defend his lands, and encouraged religious tolerance.

△ EMPEROR Shah Jehan (ruled 1627-1658) was ruthless but clever. He built the Taj Mahal.

△ AURANGZEB (ruled 1658-1707) was the last great Mogul emperor. He faced many rebellions.

◁ AFTER AKBAR died in 1605 Mogul rulers faced opposition from other Indian leaders who wanted to get rid of Mogul rule. They were Hindus and Sikhs, so did not share the Moguls' Muslim religion. In the seventeenth and eighteenth centuries there were wars between the Moguls and the Rajput and Maratha peoples and from southern Indian kingdoms like Mysore.

▷ MAP showing the migration of groups of people from the Nile area in the north and from south of the Sahara Desert.

Egypt
Arabia
Sahara Desert
Mali
Ethiopia
Ghana Benin
Somalia
Kilwa
Madagascar
Zimbabwe

△ SHIVAJI (1627-1680), king of the Marathas.

▽ TIPU, Sultan of Mysore (1749-1799).

△ TIMBUKTU was the capital city of Mansa Musa, king of Mali (died 1337). He ruled over a country that grew rich from the large quantities of gold mined there.

▽ IN 1324, King Mansa Musa went on a pilgrimage to Mecca.

△ FROM the twelfth to the fifteenth centuries, Kilwa was the leading port in East Africa. Its rulers grew rich through trade.

Many separate kingdoms flourished in Africa. Some, like the great trading cities of Gedi and Kilwa, grew up along the east coast. Their rulers were proud and powerful. On the west coast, sixteenth-century kings of Benin grew rich through selling pepper, palm oil, ivory, and slaves. Inland, great empires – Ghana, Mali, Songhai, and Kanem Borno – grew up along the southern edge of the Sahara. Farther south, around 1430, the kings of Zimbabwe built an impressive palace-city.

△ IN BENIN, the queen mother (center) trained the heir to the throne (right).

△ THE KINGS of Axum (present-day Ethiopia) claimed descent from King Solomon and the Queen of Sheba.

▷ DURING the fourth century, kings and queens of Axum built huge stone obelisks as monuments to their power.

27

RENAISSANCE EUROPE

TODAY THE RULERS of Renaissance Europe are remembered as outstanding patrons of art and architecture. Many Italian cities – such as Rome, where the popes lived, and Florence, ruled by the Medici dynasty – were transformed by beautiful new churches, palaces, banks, and libraries during the fifteenth and sixteenth centuries. Rulers paid for these fine new buildings, because they were impressive and increased their status.

▽ LORENZO DE' MEDICI, "the Magnificent," ruler of Florence from 1469-1492. He was a patron of literature and the arts, and a skilled poet.

▷ BANKERS at work in fifteenth-century Italy. One great banking family, the Medici, grew so rich and successful that they became rulers of the city-state of Florence.

◁ ITALIAN statesman Niccolo Machiavelli (1469-1527) wrote an influential book that told kings how to rule.

△ FROM the fourteenth to the sixteenth centuries, rulers in Italy paid architects to design new buildings for their cities.

▷ FEDERICO and Battista da Montefeltro ruled over the city-state of Urbino from 1444-1482.

▽ THE ITALIAN CITY of Venice became one of the centers of the Renaissance in Italy.

◁ ISABELLA D'ESTE (1474-1539), wife of the ruler of Mantua, was a great patron of the arts.

▽ THE POPE was head of the Roman Catholic Church. He also ruled lands in Italy, called the Papal States.

Some rulers, like Francesco Gonzaga of Mantua (lived 1466-1519), were also knowledgeable and scholarly.

However, many Renaissance rulers had to devote their time to war. Rebellious subjects rioted, and ambitious relatives plotted to seize power. Few rulers felt secure on their thrones. Two French kings – Henri III (ruled 1574-1589) and Henri IV (ruled 1589-1610) – were assassinated. Queen Juana "the Mad" of Castile (ruled 1505-1510) was imprisoned for life by her son. King Charles I of England (ruled 1625-1649) fought and lost a war against Parliament and was beheaded.

◁ THE RULER of the rich merchant city-state of Venice was called "the Doge." He was chosen from among the city's leading families. This is Doge Francesco Foscari (ruled 1423-1457).

QUEEN CATHERINE de' Medici ruled France on behalf of her young son from 1559-1589.

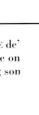

◁ IN THE sixteenth century France was divided by quarrels between Catholics and Protestants. At first Queen Catherine tried to bring peace, but later she supported the Catholics and agreed to a massacre of Protestants on St. Bartholemew's Day in 1572.

△ THE BEAUTIFUL château of Chambord, built for King François I of France (ruled 1515-1547).

◁ DIANE DE POITIERS (1519-1559) mistress of King François, and a great patron of art.

There were religious troubles for rulers as well. Henry VIII of England and several German princes quarreled dramatically with the Pope. Catholics fought Protestants on the streets of France. Scandalous church leaders, like the Spanish Pope Alexander VI (reigned 1492-1503), brought disgrace on the Church. He fathered four illegitimate children, plotted against the Italian princes, was accused of bribery and corruption, and banned books that did not follow the Church's teaching.

▷ THE SIX WIVES of King Henry VIII. Like all past queens, they could not choose their husbands. Henry chose them for his own political and personal reasons.

Catherine of Aragon (1485-1536). Divorced.

Anne Boleyn (1504-1536). Beheaded.

Jane Seymour (1509-1537). Died in childbirth.

Anne of Cleves (1515-1557). Divorced.

Catherine Howard (1520-1542). Beheaded.

Catherine Parr (1512-1548). Survived.

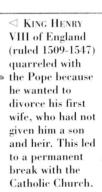

◁ KING HENRY VIII of England (ruled 1509-1547) quarreled with the Pope because he wanted to divorce his first wife, who had not given him a son and heir. This led to a permanent break with the Catholic Church.

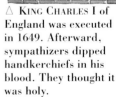

△ KING CHARLES I of England was executed in 1649. Afterward, sympathizers dipped handkerchiefs in his blood. They thought it was holy.

△ QUEEN ELIZABETH I (ruled 1558-1603) was Henry VIII's daughter. She governed England wisely and well.

◁ MARY QUEEN OF SCOTS (1542-1587) inherited the throne when she was only one week old. Her mother ruled Scotland until 1560. Mary was emotional and impulsive, and did not make a good queen. Angry Scottish nobles forced her to flee to England in 1568. There she became involved in plots against Queen Elizabeth I. As a result she was beheaded.

◁ OLIVER CROMWELL, commander of Parliament's army, ruled England from 1648-1658.

ANCIEN RÉGIME

ANCIEN RÉGIME means "the old way of ruling" – by kings with wide powers, rather than by elected representatives of the people.

During his long reign, Louis XIV of France achieved what other Ancien Régime rulers merely hoped for: unquestioned royal control of government and church. Kings and queens in Austria, Spain, Russia, and Prussia, from around 1650 to the early nineteenth century, all tried to strengthen royal government. Elector Frederick the Great of Prussia (ruled 1740-1786) and Empress Catherine of Russia (ruled 1762-1796) were strong rulers, but failed to equal what Louis XIV had done.

△ KING LOUIS XIV of France (ruled 1643-1715) once declared: "L'état, c'est moi" (I am the state).

△ QUEEN Marie Antoinette of France was the wife of King Louis XVI (below). They were both guillotined in 1793.

▷ JACQUES BRISSOT (1754-1793), led the moderate revolutionaries.

◁ MAXIMILIEN Robespierre (1758-1794), leader of the radical revolutionaries.

▽ NAPOLEON Bonaparte (ruled France 1799-1815). His greed for power led to his downfall. He died in exile in 1821.

THE HABSBURG DYNASTY

The Habsburgs were a princely German family. In 1477, they acquired vast lands in southern Europe by marriage, and by 1600 ruled over a world empire, with possessions in South America and the Far East, "on which the sun never set." They fell from power in 1918.

△ EMPEROR Franz Josef of Austria (ruled 1848-1916). His attack on Serbia helped to spark off World War I.

◁ KING PHILIP II of Spain (ruled 1556-1598) was the son of Charles V (below left). He sent the Armada to attack England in 1588.

▷ HOLY Roman Emperor Charles V (ruled 1519-1556). He ruled more land than any other European monarch.

△ KING LUDWIG II of Bavaria (in present-day Germany). He ruled 1864-1886, but was said to be mad.

▽ FREDERICK THE GREAT (ruled 1740-1786) was king of Prussia (present-day northern Germany). He worked hard to increase Prussia's power, through war and trade.

▽ TSAR Ivan IV "the Terrible" ruled Russia from 1553-1584. He made Russia strong, but was very cruel.

△ IN THE fifteenth and sixteenth centuries, Russian rulers built a splendid palace-city, called the Kremlin (fortress), in the center of Moscow. It covered 90 acres and contained two cathedrals.

Unhappily for themselves, Louis XIV's descendants, Louis XV (ruled 1715-1774) and Louis XVI (ruled 1774-1793), discovered that government controlled by a king only worked well when that king was intelligent and capable. Louis XV (known as "the Well-Loved," because he had so many mistresses) refused to listen to good advice. Louis XVI led France into an economic crisis, which helped to spark off the French Revolution of 1789. He was executed in 1793. From 1799-1815, France was ruled by Napoleon Bonaparte, a brilliant army general with ambitious plans to conquer the whole of Europe, and to rule Russia, too.

▷ EMPRESS Catherine the Great ruled Russia from 1762-1796. Her rule has caused controversy. Some historians see her as harsh and oppressive; others see her as stern but effective.

◁ QUEEN CHRISTINA of Sweden (ruled 1632-1654). She was educated like a boy and hated marriage. She abdicated in 1654 and devoted the rest of her life to religion and the arts.

△ TSAR Peter the Great of Russia (ruled 1682-1725) was 6 feet 8 inches tall. He won new lands for Russia, and built a new capital city, St. Petersburg, on the Baltic Sea.

Alone in Europe, the people of the Netherlands had no king. Their land was a republic, ruled by a "stadholder" (state guardian), elected from noble families. In 1677 Prince William of Orange, the son of Stadholder William II, married Princess Mary of England. He ruled Britain as William III from 1689 to 1702.

Ludwig II's castle of Neuschwanstein, 1869

△ EMPRESS Maria Theresa of Austria (ruled 1740-1780) and her 10 children. In 1740, she inherited vast lands from her father, Holy Roman Emperor Charles VI. Other European rulers did not want a woman to rule; this led to major international conflicts. Peace finally came in 1763.

△ PARLIAMENT invited William of Orange, son-in-law of King James II of England, to become king in 1688.

AMERICA

FROM 1492 TO 1776, the kings and queens of four European nations – Spain, Britain, Russia, and France – claimed the right to rule North America. This did not please the settlers in the American colonies. They had emigrated to America to be free to live as they chose. By the eighteenth century, they were particularly angry about having to pay British taxes, since they had no say in how Britain's government was run. This led to the American Revolution.

In 1775, armed colonists clashed with British troops at Lexington, Massachussets. On July 4, 1776, Thomas Jefferson of Virginia drew up a Declaration of Independence on behalf of all thirteen British colonies. The Declaration proclaimed that the British colonies in America were now independent, and that they would in future be governed as a republic.

△ THE FIRST Europeans in America settled in the east, in the thirteen colonies. In 1803, the government of the new United States of America purchased the huge territory of Louisiana from France.

Canada
United States
Louisiana
Mexico
South America

◁ IN 1620, Protestant pilgrims left England to set up a new community in America. They were seeking religious freedom, away from King James I and the Church of England.

◁ 102 PILGRIMS, plus crew, crossed to America on the *Mayflower*. The journey was crowded, rough, and dangerous.

△ EUROPEAN SETTLERS traded foods and furs with Native Americans, and often they fought.

Led by army commander George Washington, the settlers finally defeated the British at the battle of Yorktown in 1781.

The thirteen colonies were free, but who was to rule them? How were the new "United States of America" to be governed? In 1787, at Philadelphia, a Constitution (set of rules) was agreed. It stated that the United States was to have a president, elected every four years. He was to govern with the help of Congress (also elected), which would have two parts: a Senate and a House of Representatives. Congress would pass new laws, and a Supreme Court would guarantee that they were administered fairly.

△ KING GEORGE III of England (ruled 1760-1820). American colonists rebelled against him.

▷ IN 1775, Paul Revere (1735-1818) made a heroic ride to warn American soldiers of advancing British troops.

▷ AT THE Boston Tea Party (1773), American colonists dumped British goods in Boston Harbor, as a protest against British taxes.

△ EUROPEAN SETTLERS wanted their towns to be ruled by religious laws.

◁ THE WELL-FORTIFIED British settlement at Jamestown was built in 1607. Local laws were made by a town meeting.

A British governor

△ BRITISH SETTLEMENTS in America were colonies; they belonged to Britain and were ruled by governors.

◁ ABRAHAM LINCOLN, sixteenth president. In office 1861-1865, he worked to end slavery.

▽ CONDITIONS on plantations (estates worked by slaves) were grim. Slaves had few rights; they were property, like cattle.

The new Constitution was put into practice in 1789. George Washington was elected as first president. He was elected again in 1793. John Adams became president from 1797-1801, and Thomas Jefferson was third president from 1801-1809. Many American leaders since then have been inspired by the ideas of freedom the constitution contains.

During the nineteenth century, Native American chiefs led the fight against European settlers who wanted to take over their traditional homelands.

△ GEORGE WASHINGTON (1732-1799) led the rebel American army to victory against the British during the War of Independence (1776-1781). He helped to plan the new American constitution and was elected first president of the United States, in office 1789-1797.

△ LEADERS of the thirteen British colonies that rebelled during the American Revolution sign the Declaration of Independence on July 4, 1776.

◁ IN 1781, the American rebels allied with French soldiers to defeat the British at the Battle of Yorktown.

▽ CHIEF STANDING Bear took the U.S. government to court in 1879 to defend the rights of Native Americans and won.

▷ NATIVE AMERICAN Chief Big Foot lies dead in the snow after the Battle of Wounded Knee in 1890.

▽ FROM THE 1840s on, European-American explorers, farmers, and goldminers made the long trek to the Wild West, hoping to make their fortunes.

△ CHIEF Mahpiua Luta (Red Cloud) fought to protect the Sioux home-lands in the 1860s and 1870s.

EUROPEAN EMPIRES

TO EUROPEAN KINGS AND QUEENS, colonial empires were important. They brought profits and prestige. Low local wages, exploitation and slavery, meant that colonial products (diamonds, gold, sugar, coffee, rubber, and tea) were cheap to produce. By the nineteenth century, colonies also provided a marketplace for selling factory-made European goods. Many of these overseas empires had actually started as commercial trading enterprises run by companies like the British East India Company. In India, rivalry between the British, Dutch, and French trading companies led to the governments intervening.

△ BY 1914, European powers controlled over half of the world, through their colonies in Africa, India, the Pacific, and the Far East.

◁ COAT OF ARMS of the East India Company, 1709.

◁ BAHADUR SHAH II (ruled 1837-1857) was the last Mogul emperor of India. He was deposed by the British after the Indian Uprising of 1887, and lived the rest of his life in exile.

▷ MEMBERS of the British East India Company formed a ruling elite in India during the eighteenth and early nineteenth centuries.

▽ OFFICIAL of the British East India Company relaxing in comfort, late eighteenth century.

△ IN 1857, after insults to their religion, sepoys (Indian soldiers) employed in the East India Company's private army rioted and attacked British people in India.

▷ EUROPEAN colonial rulers were proud of their overseas empires. Queen Victoria of England was proclaimed Empress of India in 1876.

△ LOCAL WORKERS sorting newly picked leaves at a British tea plantation in the colony of Ceylon (present-day Sri Lanka), around 1900.

△ DURING the nineteenth century, many European explorers made dangerous journeys into the African interior.

△ SLAVERY was abolished in the British Empire in 1807. British antislavery patrols sailed along the coasts of Africa throughout the 19th century.

In the nineteenth century, there was a "scramble for Africa." After explorers publicized the rich resources there, Europeans seized control.

It took centuries before most colonies were free. India did not win freedom until 1947, and many African colonies did not become independent until the 1960s. South American colonies, however, had broken away from Spain by 1823.

◁ LOUIS BOTHA, first prime minister (1910-1919) of the new Union of South Africa, formed from Dutch and British colonies.

△ RIVAL BRITISH and Dutch colonists (known as the Boers, or farmers) fought against each other in 1880-1881 and 1889-1902. British troops were led by General Kitchener; the Boers were led by General Botha.

◁ CECIL RHODES was prime minister of Britain's Cape Colony (part of present-day South Africa) 1890-1896. He played an important part in the Boer War, and encouraged exploration, British conquests, and trade.

Zulu warriors

△ IN 1879, British colonial troops in South Africa fought against Zulu warriors led by King Cetewayo (ruled 1872-1879). At first, the Zulus were victorious, at the battles of Isandlhwana and Rorke's Drift. But they were defeated by the British at Ulundi, and King Cetewayo was exiled.

▷ EMPEROR Maximilian of Mexico (ruled 1864-1867) was executed by firing squad after being captured by rebel soldiers.

◁ JOSÉ DE SAN MARTIN fought to free Argentina and Chile from Spanish rule. They both became independent – Argentina in 1810, Chile in 1818.

▷ SIMON BOLIVAR (1783-1830) known as "the Liberator" led successful campaigns for independence from Spanish colonial rule in Ecuador, Venezuela, Colombia, and Peru.

▷ EMPEROR Pedro II of Brazil (ruled 1831-1889). Brazil was a former Portuguese colony, and Pedro was a member of the Portuguese royal family, who had fled there to escape Napoleon in 1809.

POWER FOR THE PEOPLE

EVER SINCE THE MIDDLE AGES, people in Europe had complained about their kings and queens. But until the American Revolution of 1776 (page 32) and the French Revolution of 1789 (page 31) few people questioned monarchy as a system of government. In the nineteenth century views began to change, although there were still some popular, capable kings and queens. Hereditary monarchs were becoming less important, as parliaments and elected ministers played an increasing part in the government of European states. Ordinary people, too, began to demand the right to vote, and to have a say in ruling their own lives.

△ KING GEORGE III of England (ruled 1760-1820) was eager to play an active part in government, but often provoked controversy. He quarreled with his prime minister, William Pitt the Younger, on many issues.

△ FROM 1810-1820, Prince George, "Prince Regent," ruled England after his father, King George III, went mad. He was king (George IV) from 1820-1830.

◁ FRANCIS II of Austria (lived 1768-1835) was made to give up the title of Holy Roman Emperor after his army was defeated by Napoleon at Austerlitz in 1805.

◁ KING LOUIS-PHILIPPE of France (ruled 1830-1848) was known as the "citizen king" because he sided with the people at the start of the French Revolution in 1789.

△ KAISER WILHELM II of Germany (ruled 1888-1918) followed aggressive foreign policies which eventually led to the outbreak of World War I.

▷ AUSTRIAN PRINCE Metternich (lived 1773-1859) was one of the most powerful conservative politicians in Europe.

▷ ARTHUR WELLESLEY, Duke of Wellington (lived 1769-1852) was a brilliant soldier. Later he became a politician. He resigned as prime minister after quarrels over how to reform Parliament.

△ KING WILLIAM IV of England (ruled 1830-1837) was known as the "sailor king" because he served in the navy. He agreed to many liberal reforms and was popular with the people.

◁ QUEEN VICTORIA of England (ruled 1837-1901) lived to see three generations of male heirs to the throne. They all ruled, in turn, after her death: her son, Edward VII (top right); her grandson, George V (left); her great-grandson, Edward VIII (bottom right).

△ BENJAMIN DISRAELI (lived 1804-1881) was a novelist and a Conservative politician. He was British prime minister in 1868, and from 1874-1880.

△ DAVID LLOYD GEORGE (lived 1863-1945), British prime minister from 1916-1922. He negotiated independence from Britain for the Irish Free State (now the Republic of Ireland) in 1921.

△ KARL MARX (lived 1818-1883) historian and philosopher. In 1848 he published the Communist Manifesto, which criticized existing governments, and called for new communist states.

△ IN 1848, there were riots and revolutions in many European states, as ordinary people demanded better, fairer, less corrupt government, and the chance to vote. In Paris, crowds burned the king's throne, and there was fighting in the streets.

▷ TSAR NICHOLAS II of Russia (ruled 1894-1917) and his family. He started a disastrous war against Japan, and failed to solve Russia's serious economic problems. In 1905 Russian people demanded civil rights but Nicholas refused to give them any real power. In 1917, led by communists, they rebelled again. Nicholas and his family were murdered in 1918.

◁ OTTO VON BISMARCK (lived 1815-1898) was chief minister of Prussia (north Germany). He led Prussia to victory in wars against France, Denmark and Austria, and proclaimed the German Empire in 1871.

▷ IN 1912 and 1913 there were two Balkan wars against Ottoman Turkey. The Balkans are an area bordering the Mediterranean Sea, including Albania, Bulgaria, Greece, Romania, part of Turkey, and the former Yugoslavia.

▷ VLADIMIR ILYICH LENIN (lived 1870-1924), leader of the 1917 Revolution in Russia. He became head of the first Soviet (communist) government of Russia in 1917.

▽ IN JUNE 1914 a Serbian nationalist named Gavrilo Princip shot dead Archduke Franz Ferdinand, heir to the Austro-Hungarian Empire, as he visited Sarajevo. This led to a political crisis in Europe and sparked off World War I (1914-1918).

▷ KARL I OF AUSTRIA (ruled 1916-1918), last emperor of the Austro-Hungarian Empire, which collapsed at the end of World War I. He was forced to give up his throne, and died in exile. Austria and Hungary became separate nations.

▽ IN 1917 Russia had two communist revolutions. The first, in February, removed Tsar Nicholas II from the throne, and set up a temporary government. In October, Bolshevik workers (hard-liners), soldiers, and sailors seized power and formed a government run on communist principles.

▷ IN 1922 Kemal Ataturk became the first president of Turkey, in office until 1938. He was strong and sometimes ruthless. He aimed to modernize and westernize Turkey after centuries of rule by the Ottomans.

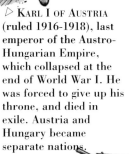

GREAT DICTATORS

△ RUSSIAN DICTATOR Joseph Stalin (ruled 1924-1953). He was cruel and ruthless; he murdered his critics and sent millions of so-called "enemies of the people" to die in labor camps.

BY THE MIDDLE of the twentieth century, in many parts of the world, kings and queens had disappeared. They had been replaced, sometimes by democratically elected presidents or prime ministers, and sometimes by dictators.

Dictators are men and women who take control of governments and run them single-handed. They have been called "great" – but only because they had so much power. Dictators are often cruel and ruthless, abolishing civil rights, ignoring (or bullying) parliaments, and forbidding criticism.

▽ IN 1928, Stalin launched collective farming. Peasants were forced to give up their own farms and work together. As a result, many starved.

▽ HITLER'S supporters, called Nazis, chose the ancient swastika symbol as their badge. It always appeared on the banners and uniforms of the Nazis.

▷ GENERALISSIMO Francisco Franco, Fascist dictator of Spain from the end of the Spanish Civil War in 1939 until his death in 1975.

▷ SIR WINSTON CHURCHILL (lived 1874-1965), soldier, journalist, and politician. From 1940-1945, he was prime minister, leading Britain to victory in World War II.

△ ADOLF HITLER (lived 1889-1945) reorganized the German National Socialist (Nazi) Party in 1920. He was chancellor of Germany from 1933 until his death in 1945.

◁ LEADERS like Hitler and Mussolini organized vast rallies of supporters. Crowds became excited and hysterical as they listened to powerful speeches and stirring music, and watched mass parades.

▽ GENERAL CHARLES DE GAULLE (lived 1890-1970), leader of the Free French opposition to the Nazis during World War II, and president of France 1959-1969. He also played a leading part in the European Common Market (now the European Union).

◁ BENITO MUSSOLINI (lived 1883-1945), Fascist dictator in Italy from 1922 until 1943. He supported Franco and Hitler (who had similar political beliefs).

Some dictators, like Argentinian Juan Perón (ruled 1943-1955 and 1973-1974), stole vast sums of money from the state. Many encouraged genocide. Over five million Jewish people died as part of Hitler's "final solution" (scheme for ethnic cleansing in Germany, 1939-1945). During Pol Pot's regime in Kampuchea (1975-1979), almost three million civilians were killed.

Perhaps rather surprisingly, many dictators started their political careers with good intentions. They often held extreme political views: ultra-nationalist, Fascist, or hardline Communist. But they came to power at times of national crisis, believing that only they knew how to solve their country's problems. Even so, it is impossible to justify their brutal behavior. The careers of other great twentieth-century "crisis leaders," for example Britain's Winston Churchill and General Charles de Gaulle in France, show that strong leadership can be combined with freedom, fairness, and respect for the law.

△ MAO ZHEDONG, Communist leader of China 1949-1976. He aimed to modernize Chinese farming, industry, and education, but his policies were harsh and caused much suffering.

◁ FRANKLIN D. ROOSEVELT, twenty-third president of the United States (1933-1945). In the 1930s, he planned a "New Deal" to bring economic recovery. After 1941 he led America in the fight against Hitler and his allies in Italy and Japan.

◁ CIXI (lived 1835-1908) was the last empress of China. From 1862 she ruled on behalf of her son, and refused to give up power even after his death in 1875. She refused to listen to demands for reform.

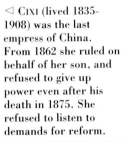

▷ SADDAM HUSSEIN (born 1935), president of Iraq since 1979. He has been criticized for his support of terrorism, his attacks on minority groups (Kurds and Marsh Arabs), and his invasion of Kuwait in 1990.

△ EVA PERÓN, called Evita (lived 1919-1952). Actress and wife of Argentinian president Juan Perón, she became very popular among poor people, and used this to further her husband's career.

A Nazi party rally

◁ YUGOSLAVIAN Marshal Josep Tito (lived 1892-1980). He fought against Hitler's German army during World War II. From 1953-1980, he was communist president of Yugoslavia.

◁ EMPEROR HIROHITO of Japan (ruled 1926-1989). After Japan was defeated in World War II, he gave up his traditional godlike status.

△ IN AFGHANISTAN in the early 1980s a civil war developed when the U.S.S.R. intervened in the country's politics. Muslim guerrillas fought against Soviet forces from camps in the mountains.

POST-WAR WORLD

F ROM 1945 TO THE 1980s, the world was dominated by two huge superpowers, the U.S. and the U.S.S.R. They held hostile political views and were armed with deadly nuclear weapons. Together with their allies, they controlled the fragile balance of power. The superpowers' leaders were the mightiest men on earth.

Leaders of smaller, less influential countries also faced major tasks. In Africa, campaigners led black peoples to freedom from European colonial rule. In Southeast Asia, politicians promoted rapid economic development. In the Middle East, after years of conflict, leaders are trying to bring peace. Religious leaders have also played an important part in twentieth-century politics.

Attlee (U.K.)
Truman (U.S.)
Stalin (U.S.S.R.)

▽ AT THE END of World War II, British, American, and Russian leaders met at Potsdam to discuss new boundaries for East European states.

◁ NIKITA KRUSCHEV (lived 1894-1971), leader of the U.S.S.R. from 1953-1964. He criticized Stalin, crushed nationalist movements in Hungary (1956) and other lands, and steadily opposed the U.S.

◁ JOHN F. KENNEDY (lived 1917-1963), thirty-fifth president of the U.S. He won a "war of nerves" against the U.S.S.R. over missile bases in Cuba in 1962.

△ FIDEL CASTRO (born 1927), communist leader of the Cuban revolution (1958) and president of Cuba since 1959. During the Cold War, Cuba was supported by the U.S.S.R.

△ MIKHAIL GORBACHEV (left, born 1931), leader of the U.S.S.R. 1985-1991. He introduced policies of perestroika (reform) and glasnost (openness). Ronald Reagan (right, born 1911), fortieth president of the U.S. At first anti-Russian, he joined with Gorbachev to negotiate arms limitation agreements.

SOLIDARNOŚĆ

△ BORIS YELTSIN (born 1931), head of state of Russia since the fall of Gorbachev and the breakup of the U.S.S.R.

△ LECH WALESA (born 1943), Polish trade unionist and leader of the Solidarity movement, which campaigned for an end to old-style communist rule. He became president of Poland in 1990.

△ VLADIMIR ZHIRINOVSKY (born 1946), outspoken leader of Russian nationalists.

△ JAWAHARLAL NEHRU (left, lived 1889-1964), first prime minister of independent India from 1947-1964. Lord Mountbatten (right, lived 1900-1979). Last viceroy (imperial governor) of India.

◁ MAHATMA (great soul) Gandhi (1869-1948), leader of non-violent campaigns for Indian independence from British rule.

▷ SINCE 1945, there have been many successful campaigns for independence by former European colonies, in Africa, South Asia and the Far East.

Kenya

Jomo Kenyatta (1891-1978)

Zimbabwe

Robert Mugabe (born 1924)

Zambia

Kenneth Kaunda (born 1924)

South Africa

Nelson Mandela (born 1918)

POST-COLONIAL LEADERS

▷ THE UNITED NATIONS organization was set up in 1945 to maintain international peace and security, to develop international friendship, and to promote human rights. Delegates from almost all nations meet regularly to discuss world problems. They often quarrel, and the United Nations (UN) is often criticized for its weakness and slowness to act. But most people agree that it is better than nothing, and hope that it may one day improve.

◁ TROOPS seconded to the United Nations act as peacekeepers in civil wars.

◁ THROUGH its agencies UNICEF (for children), UNHCR (for refugees), and WHO (for health) the UN aims to help poor and sick people.

MIDDLE EASTERN LEADERS

Cyprus

Archbishop Makarios (1913-1977)

Egypt

Anwar Sadat (1918-1981)

Libya

Muammar Gadhafi (born 1942)

Palestine

Yasir Arafat (born 1929)

△ THERE has been constant tension in the Middle East in the twentieth century.

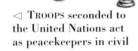

Israel

Golda Meir (in office 1969-1974)

Indira Gandhi (in office 1966-1977, 1980-1984)

India

Benazir Bhutto (in office 1988-1990, 1993-present)

Pakistan

Margaret Thatcher (in office 1979-1990)

U.K.

△ FROM THE 1950s to the 1970s, courageous leaders of minority groups in many countries campaigned for equal civil rights. One of the most famous and influential campaigners was African-American Dr. Martin Luther King, Jr. (1929-1968).

△ THE LATE twentieth century saw women slowly being elected to positions of power in many countries.

▽ MUHAMMAD Reza Shah Pahlavi (ruled 1941-1979), last emperor of Iran.

△ FAISAL IBN ABD AL-AZIZ (lived 1900-1975), king of Saudi Arabia. With other Arab leaders, he ruled over a region that rapidly became prosperous as oil prices rose.

△ IN 1979, Ayatollah Khomeini (lived 1900-1989) became head of state in Iran. He introduced strict laws based on the traditional teachings of Islam.

PAST AND FUTURE

COMPARED WITH PAST KINGS AND QUEENS, today's royal families have little political power. A few still maintain the old traditions, but many are eager to modernize the way they live. They train for professions or do voluntary work. They even make use of their families' history, "selling" it like any other workers in the heritage industry.

Rulers have always tried to manipulate their image. They have ordered flattering portraits, tactful biographies, and sympathetic histories of their reigns. Only a few, like Oliver Cromwell, the seventeenth-century English Puritan leader, have dared to appear in public "warts and all." Even so, their reputations have depended on their achievement.

△ GOLD MASK found at Mycenae, Greece, made around 1500 B.C. It portrays an unidentified king.

◁ ROMAN RULERS were often portrayed in lifelike stone carvings. These can give us an insight into a ruler's character, even after almost 2000 years. This portrait carving shows Julius Caesar (lived 100-44 B.C.).

▷ THIS Roman mosaic shows Alexander the Great of Macedon (lived 356-323 B.C.).

◁ THROUGHOUT the centuries, rulers have commissioned grand and imposing monuments to impress onlookers with their magnificence and power.

◁ IMAGE-CONSCIOUS rulers like Queen Elizabeth I of England (ruled 1558-1603) commissioned many copies of "official" portraits, so their subjects could see them at their best.

▷ IN RECENT years, young, good-looking, well-dressed leaders have become "media darlings." Because they appear so attractive in photographs and on television, their image can seem more important than their actions.

President Kennedy

Princess Diana

◁ TO CREATE a good public image, some leaders have tried to hide their past mistakes or illegal actions. When it was discovered that President Nixon (in office 1969-1974) had covered up evidence of a burglary of his opponents' offices, he was forced to resign.

▷ LUCREZIA BORGIA (lived 1480-1519) was falsely accused of being a poisoner. Her family's enemies knew this would cause trouble for her powerful male relatives.

◁ RULERS who fell from power – like French emperor Napoleon (ruled 1799-1815), seen here in exile – were used by writers as warnings of what might happen if pride and ambition ran out of control.

△ RULERS told artists what they wanted their tombs to look like while they were still alive. This tomb portrays Spanish noble Martin Vaquez de Arce around 1486.

▽ RULERS who failed politically might later be honored because of their beliefs. King Charles I of England, executed 1649, is seen by some people as a saint.

Today, some people suspect that a ruler's appearance is becoming more important than what they actually achieve. This seems to be true for democratically elected leaders, as well as for hereditary kings and queens. John F. Kennedy was voted president in 1960 partly because he looked better on television than Richard Nixon, his rival. In the 1980s, glamorous press photographs of Princess Diana made the British royal family very popular, but by the 1990s scandalous newspaper stories about her had seriously damaged its prestige. Is this media power good or bad? Will it change the way we are ruled?

▽ IN THE FUTURE, kings and queens might earn money by showing curious tourists around their own stately homes.

▷ A RULER'S RELATIONS with the media – books, newspapers, and television – are now all-important.

▷ FOR CENTURIES, politicians and rulers in many lands have used spies and secret police to keep their subjects under control. Now, with modern electronic technology, it may prove possible for unpopular rulers to retreat inside fortified control towers, running their countries by remote control and keeping their enemies at bay.

△ PRINCE CHARLES, heir to the throne in Britain, goes "walkabout" with his son Prince William, the next in line to the throne. In the past, the right to rule in most royal families descended from father to son. A daughter could only rule as queen if she had no brothers. Even then, many people disapproved. Today, in some countries, for example, Sweden, this old rule has been changed.

▷ MEMBERS of many modern royal families have studied for other professions. For example, Emperor Hirohito of Japan (ruled 1926-1989) was also a marine biologist.

▷ FOR YEARS, members of royal families have acted as patrons of charities and other good causes. A few, like Princess Anne of the U.K. (born 1950), now play a much more active role.

TIMELINE

Note: Unless otherwise stated, the dates refer to the time when a ruler was in power or held office.

B.C.
c. 2500 Prince Gilgamesh of Sumer.
1792-1750 King Hammurabi of Babylon.
1766-1122 Shang emperors rule China.
c. 1500 King of Hsia, and first emperor of China.
1489-1469 Queen Hatshepsut of Egypt.
1370-1353 Pharaoh Akenaton of Egypt and Queen Nefertiti.
1352-1343 Pharaoh Tutankhamen of Egypt.
1290-1224 Pharaoh Ramses II of Egypt.
c. 1270 Queen Nefertari of Egypt.
c. 974-937 King Solomon of Israel.
721-711 King Evil-Merodach of Sumer.
c. 621 Draco, archon of Athens.
594 Solon, archon of Athens.
510 (deposed) King Tarquin of Rome.
c. 495-429 (lived) Pericles, leader of Athens.
384-322 (lived) Demosthenes of Athens.
336-330 King Darius of Persia.

King Darius of Persia

336-323 (ruled) Alexander the Great of Macedon.
221-206 Emperor Qin Shi Huangdi of China.

106-48 (lived) Pompey, leader of the Roman Republic.
100-44 (lived) Julius Caesar, leader of the Roman Republic.
69-30 (lived) Mark Antony, leader of the Roman Republic
48-30 Cleopatra VII of Egypt.
46 (died) King Vercingetorix of the Gauls.
27 B.C.-A.D. 14 Octavian rules as Emperor Augustus of Rome.

A.D.
14-37 Emperor Tiberius of Rome.
54-68 Emperor Nero of Rome.
62 (died) Queen Boudicca of the Iceni.
54 King Ambiorix of the Gauls fought the Romans.
98-117 Emperor Trajan of Rome.
117-138 Emperor Hadrian of Rome.
284-305 Emperor Diocletian of Rome.
306-337 Emperor Constantine, ruler of the eastern Roman empire, now called Byzantium.
c. 406-453 Attila, leader of the Huns.
471-526 Emperor Theodoric of Byzantium.
475-476 Emperor Romulus Augustulus of Rome.
527-565 Emperor Justinian of Byzantium (with Empress Theodora, 527-547).
c. 570-632 (lived) The Prophet Muhammad, first leader of the Muslims.
626 (died) King Redwald of East Anglia.

King Charlemagne of the Franks

626-649 Emperor Tang Tai-tsung of China.
632-634 Caliph Abu Bakr.
634-644 Caliph Umar.
685-705 Caliph Abd al-Malik.
771-814 King Charlemagne of the Franks.
780-803 Empress Irene of Byzantium.
786-809 Caliph Harun al-Rashid.
871-899 King Alfred the Great of Wessex.
874-861 Caliph al-Mutawakkil.
907 (died) Sultan Ismail Samanid.
919-936 King Henry the Fowler of Saxony.
936-973 Holy Roman Emperor Otto the Great.
978-1015 Prince Vladimir I (the Great) of Kiev, Russia.
950-985 King Harald Bluetooth of Norway.
983-1002 King Otto III of Germany.
1039-1046 King Henry III of Germany.
1042-1066 King Edward the Confessor of England.
1066-1087 King William I of England, the Conqueror.
1105-1154 King Roger II of Sicily.
1122-1204 (lived) Queen Eleanor of Aquitaine.
1126-1160 Queen Melisende of Jerusalem.

1137-1193 Sultan Salah al-Din (Saladin), leader of Muslims in the Holy Land and Egypt.
1152-1190 King Frederick I Barbarossa of Germany.
1154-1189 Henry II of England.
1189-1199 King Richard the Lionheart of England.
1192 Shoguns begin to rule in Japan.
1206-1227 Genghis Khan, Mongol leader.
1207-1231 (lived) Princess Elizabeth of Hungary.
1213-1276 King Jaime I of Aragon.
1226-1270 King Louis IX of France.
1226-1234 Blanche of Castile, queen of France.
1272-1307 King Edward I of England.
1281-1324 Ottoman Sultan Uthman.
1306-1329 King Robert the Bruce of Scotland.
1327-1387 King Edward III of England.
1332 (died) King Mansa Musa of Mali.
1364-1380 King Charles V of France.
1367-1387 Aztec Tlatoani Acamapichti.
1368-1398 Emperor Chu Yuan-chang of China.

1369-1405 Timur (Tamerlane), Mongol leader.
1394-1460 (lived) Prince Henry the Navigator of Portugal.
1417-1426 Aztec Tlatoani Chimalpopoca.
1413-1422 King Henry V of England.
1416-1458 King Alfonso the Magnanimous of Aragon.
1422-1471 King Henry VI of England.
1449-1453 Emperor Constantine XI of Byzantium.
1451-1481 Ottoman Sultan Mehmet II.
1469-1492 Lorenzo

King Alfonso the Magnanimous

de' Medici, the Magnificent, ruler of Florence.
1479-1504 King Ferdinand and Queen Isabella of Spain.
1483-1485 King Richard III of England.
1485-1536 (lived) Catherine of Aragon, queen of England.
1492-1503 Pope Alexander VI.
1502-1520 Aztec Tlatoani Montezuma II.
1504-1536 (lived) Anne Boleyn, queen of England.
1509-1537 (lived) Jane Seymour, queen of England.
1509-1547 King Henry VIII of England.
1512-1548 (lived) Catherine Parr, queen of England.

Alexander the Great

Catherine the Great

1515-1547 King
François I of France.
1515-1557 (lived)
Anne of Cleves, queen
of England.
1519-1556 Holy
Roman Emperor
Charles V.
1520-1542 (lived)
Catherine Howard,
queen of England.
1520-1566 Ottoman
Sultan Suleyman the
Magnificent.
1526-1530 Mogul
Emperor Babur.
1530-1556 Mogul
Emperor Humayun.
1542-1587 Mary
Queen of Scots.
1553-1558 Queen
Mary I of England.
1553-1584 Tsar Ivan
the Terrible of Russia.
1556-1598 King
Philip II of Spain.
1556-1605 Mogul
Emperor Akbar.
1558-1603 Queen
Elizabeth I of England.
1559-1589 Queen
Catherine de Medici of
France.
1574-1589 King
Henri III of France.
1574-1595 Seljuk
Sultan Murad III.
1589-1610 King
Henri IV of France.
1603-1625 King
James I of England and
Scotland.
1603-1868 Tokugawa
dynasty of shoguns,
rulers of Japan.
1605-1627 Mogul
Emperor Jehangir.
1625-1649 King
Charles I of England.
1627-1658 Mogul
Emperor Shah Jehan.
1627-1680 Shivaji,
leader of the Marathas.
1643-1715 King Louis
XIV of France.
1658-1707 Mogul
Emperor Aurangzeb.
1682-1725 Tsar Peter
the Great of Russia.

1689-1702 King
William III of England.
1732-1799 (lived)
George Washington,
president of the U.S.
1740-1780 Empress
Maria Theresa of
Austria.
1740-1786 King
Frederick the Great of
Prussia.
1749-1799 Sultan
Tipu of Mysore.
1760-1820 King
George III of Britain.
1762-1796 Empress
Catherine the Great of
Russia.
1769-1852 (lived)
Duke of Wellington,
prime minister of
Britain.
1774-1793 King Louis
XVI of France.
1797-1801 President
John Adams of the U.S.
1799-1815 Napoleon
Bonaparte, emperor of
France.
1801-1809 President
Thomas Jefferson of
the U.S.
1804-1881 (lived)
Benjamin Disraeli,
prime minister of
Britain.
1810-1820 George,
prince regent of Britain
(King George IV 1820-
1830).
1815-1898 Otto von
Bismarck, chief
minister of Prussia.
1829-1909 (lived)
Geronimo (Goyathlay),
Native American
leader.
1830-1848 King Louis
Philippe of France.
c. 1834-1890 (lived)
Sitting Bull, Native
American leader.
1837-1901 Queen
Victoria of Britain.
1841-1929 (lived)
Georges Clemenceau,
prime minister of
France.
1848-1916 Emperor
Franz Josef of Austria.
1859-1941 (lived)
Kaiser Wilhelm II of
Germany.
1861-1865 President
Abraham Lincoln of
U.S.
1862-1908 Empress
Cixi of China.

1864-1886 King
Ludwig II of Bavaria.
1865-1901 King
Leopold II of Belgium.
1869-1948 (lived)
Mohandas "Mahatma"
Gandhi, leader of
struggle for Indian
independence.
1870-1924 (lived)
Vladimir Ilyich Lenin,
Russian Communist
leader.
1872-1879 Zulu King
Cetewayo.
1874-1965 (lived)
Winston Churchill,
prime minister of
Britain.
1882-1945 (lived)
President Franklin D.
Roosevelt of the U.S.
1889-1964 (lived)
Jawaharlal Nehru,
prime minister of
India.

Queen Victoria

1890-1896 Cecil
Rhodes, prime
minister of Cape Colony.
1890-1970 (lived)
Charles de Gaulle,
president of France.
1891-1978 (lived)
Jomo Kenyatta,
President of Kenya.
1892-1980 (lived)
Josep Tito, leader of
former Yugoslavia.

1894-1971 (lived)
Nikita Khruschev,
leader of the U.S.S.R.
1894-1917 Tsar
Nicholas II of Russia.
1900-1989 (lived)
Ayatollah Khomeini of
Iran.
1910-1919 Louis
Botha, prime minister
of South Africa.
1911 (born) President
Ronald Reagan of the
U.S.
1913-1977 (lived)
Archbishop Makarios,
leader of Greek
Cypriots.
1916-1918 Emperor
Karl I of Austria.
1916-1922 David
Lloyd George, prime
minister of Britain.
1917-1963 (lived)
President John F.
Kennedy of the U.S.
1918 (born) Nelson
Mandela, president of
South Africa.
1918-1981 Anwar
Sadat, president of
Egypt.
1919-1952
(lived) Eva Perón,
co-ruler of
Argentina.

1922-1938 Kemal
Ataturk, president of
Turkey.
1922-1943 Benito
Mussolini, dictator of
Italy.
1924 (born) Kenneth
Kaunda, president of
Zambia.
1924 (born) Robert
Mugabe, prime minister
of Zimbabwe.

1924-1953 Josef
Stalin, dictator of
the U.S.S.R.
1926-1989 Emperor
Hirohito of Japan.

Josef Stalin

1927 (born) President
Fidel Castro of Cuba.
1929 (born) Yasir
Arafat, leader of
Palestine.
1931 (born) Mikhail
Gorbachev, former
leader of the U.S.S.R.
1931 (born) Boris
Yeltsin, president of
Russia.
1933-1945 Adolf
Hitler, dictator of
Germany.
1937 (born) Saddam
Hussein, ruler of Iraq.
1939-1975 Francisco
Franco, dictator of
Spain.
1941-1979
Muhammad Reza
Pahlavi, shah of Iran.
1942 (born) Muammar
Gadhafi, leader of
Libya.
1949-1976 Mao
Zhedong, ruler of
China.
1969-1974 Richard
Nixon, president of the
U.S.
1969-1974 Golda
Meir, prime minister of
Israel.
**1966-1977, 1980-
1984** Indira Gandhi,
prime minister of India.
1979-1990 Margaret
Thatcher, prime
minister of Britain.

Shivaji of the Marathas

GLOSSARY

Abdicate Give up the throne.

Aediles Roman government officials in charge of water supplies and public health.

Apotheosis The ceremony after the death of a Roman emperor when he was transformed into a god.

Archons Government officials in Athens, ancient Greece.

Assassinate To murder someone for political reasons.

Bolsheviks A group of political activists who wanted a revolution in the way pre-1917 Russia was governed, and were prepared to use violence if necessary.

Boulé A council of leading citizens in Athens.

Caliphs Rulers of Muslim lands in the Middle East and North Africa during the Middle Ages.

Censors Roman government officials who collected data about the population.

Colony Part of the world ruled by a foreign power for its own benefit, often with little consideration for the native inhabitants.

Consuls Top government officials in the Roman republic. Two were appointed every year to lead the government.

Democracy A form of government run "by the people, for the people."

Dictator A ruler who has absolute power.

Deposed Removed from the throne by force.

Duma The Russian parliament in the nineteenth century.

Dynasty Ruling family.

Elite Either "the best" or the "upper classes."

Exiled Forced to leave one's homeland and live abroad.

Fascism A political theory popular with twentieth-century dictators. It says that the state should have complete control over individuals, and that violence can be used by rulers to achieve this.

Feudal A form of government popular in medieval Europe. Kings gave lands to nobles in return for support; nobles gave land to peasants in return for their work.

Forum The central market in Rome, and an important meeting place.

Guillotine A machine used in the French Revolution to cut off peoples' heads. It was designed to be kinder than hanging.

Jarl Viking lord, land owner, and war leader.

Monarchy Rule by kings and queens.

Mongol Nomadic people from Central Asia who invaded the Middle East and Eastern Europe in the Middle Ages.

Nationalism A political theory that demands the right for the people of a nation to govern themselves, free from foreign control.

Nazi Member of the German Fascist party (powerful 1930s-1940s) led by Adolf Hitler.

Oppressive Stern and heavy-handed.

Pagan Someone who does not believe in the Jewish, Christian, or Muslim faiths.

Partisans Freedom-fighters who fought against the Nazi invasion of Yugoslavia during the World War II.

Patricians Nobles in ancient Rome.

Patron Someone who supports an artist by gifts of money and by encouragement and praise.

Persecuted Punished because of religious or political beliefs.

Pectoral Jewelry worn on the chest.

Pilgrim Someone who makes a journey for religious reasons, for example, the Puritan families who emigrated from Britain to America in the early seventeenth century.

Plague A deadly, infectious disease, carried by rat fleas.

Plebeians The ordinary people in Rome.

Praetors Judges in Rome.

Prophet Person who believes he or she has a message from God.

Protestants Christians who organized their own new church in the sixteenth century, after religious and political quarrels with the Roman Catholic Church.

Pueblo Native American village, built in southwestern regions. Composed of several small houses, all joined together, and run as a community.

Qipu Inca document, made of knotted string. Qipus recorded weights, measures, and other important things.

Radical Wanting thorough change.

Republic A form of government without a king or queen. Republics often elect presidents as heads of state.

Samurai Japanese warrior nobleman.

Shariyah Muslim law, based on the Koran.

Shoguns Top Japanese generals, in charge of the government from twelfth to nineteenth centuries.

Stadholder Leader of the Dutch Republic from the sixteenth to eighteenth centuries.

Sultan Medieval Turkish word for prince or ruler.

Tatars Central Asian nation, often at war with Russia in the past, sometimes also known as "Tartars."

Tlatoani The Aztec ruler.

Tsar The Russian ruler.

Tyrant A strong person in charge of the government. Originally (in ancient Greece) an honorable title. Today, often used to mean dictator.

INDEX

Entries is bold refer to illustrations.

A

Africa 7, 9, **18**, 34, **35**, 40
  North 10, 18, 26, 27
  rulers of 27, **27**, **35**, 40
  southern 27, **27**, 35
Akenaton, pharaoh of Egypt **8**
Alexander the Great **11**, 42
Alfred the Great **15**, 20
America, North 20, 25, **25**, 32, 36; *see also* U.S.
  South 24, 25, **30**, 35, 39, **39**
ancient world, rulers of 6, **6**, 7, **7**, 8, **8**, 9, **9**
Anglo-Saxons 15, 20
Aragon 19, **20**
Athens 11, **11**
Attila the Hun 15
Augustus, Roman emperor 13
Austria 30, **30**, 31, 36, **36**, 37
  rulers of **30**, 31, 36
Aztecs 24, **24**

B

Baghdad 16, **17**, 26
Balkans, the 37
Bosnia 26
Boudicca, queen of the Iceni 14
Britain 13, 15, 31, 32, **33**, 34, **35**, 36, **37**, 38, **43**; *see also* England
Byzantine Empire **18**, 19, **19**, 21, 26
  rulers of **19**, **20**, **21**

C

Caesar, Julius 12, **12**, 13, 14, 42
caliphs 16, **16**, 17, 26
Cambodia 23, **23**, 39
Castile 20, 28
Catherine de' Medici, queen of France **29**
Catherine the Great, empress of Russia 31
Catholics, Roman 19, 28, 29, **29**
Celts 14, **14**, 15
Charlemagne, king of the Franks 15
Charles I, king of England 28, **29**, 42
China 22, **22**, 23, **23**
  rulers of 22, **22**, 23, **39**

Christians 13, 14, 17, **18**, 20; *see also* Catholics, Roman, religion, Protestants
city-states 7, 10, **10**, 11, **11**, 28
Cleopatra VII, queen of Egypt 9, **12**
Communists 37, 39, **39**, 40
Constantine, Roman emperor 13
Constantinople 19, 26
Cromwell, Oliver 29, 42

D

Darius, king of Persia 9
Declaration of Independence 32
democracy 11, **11**
Denmark 15, 18, 37
dictators 38, **38**, 39, **39**

E

Edward the Confessor, king of England **15**
Egypt 8, **11**, 20
  rulers of 8, **8**, 9, **12**
Elizabeth I, queen of England **29**, 34, 42
England 13, 14, 15, 19, **20**; *see also* Britain
  rulers of **8**, 9, **12**, 15, 19, 21, 28, **29**, 32, 34, **36**, 43
Europe 11, 14, **14**, 15, **15**, 18, **18**, 19, **19**, 28, **28**, 30, 31, **31**, 32, 33, 34, 35, 36, 37

F

Far East 22, 23, 30, 34, **34**, 40
France 14, 15, 19, 29, 31, 32, **32**, **33**, 34, 37
  rulers of **15**, **20**, 21, 28, **29**, 30, **30**, 31, 32, 36, **38**, 39
Franks 14, **14**, 15
Frederick the Great, king of Prussia 31
French Revolution 30, 31, 36, **36**

G

Gaulle, Charles de 38, 39
Genghis Khan 23
Germany **6**, 31, 37, 39
  rulers of **18**, 19, **19**, 20, 29, 30, 31, 36, 37, 38, 39
Greece 10, **10**, 11, **11**, 37, 42

H

Hadrian, Roman emperor **13**
Hapsburgs 30
Hatshepsut, queen of Egypt **8**, 9
Henry VIII, king of England 29, **29**
Hitler, Adolf 38, 39, **39**
Holy Roman Emperors 19, 20, 21, **30**, **31**, 36
Hungary 19, **21**, 26, 37, 40

I

Incas 24, **24**
India 26, **26**, 34, 35
  rulers of **26**, 34, **35**, 40, 41
Iran 9, 19, 26, 41; *see also* Persia
Iraq 7, **16**, 17, 19, 39
Islam 16, **16**, 17, **17**, 41
Istanbul 17, **18**, 26
Italy 15, **18**, 28; *see also* Roman Empire
  rulers of **18**, 28, **28**, 29, **38**; *see also* Roman emperors
Ivan the Terrible, tsar of Russia **31**

J, L

Japan 23, **23**, 37, 39
  rulers of 23, **23**, **39**, 43
Jerusalem 9, **17**, 21
Jews 9, 17, 20, 39

Lenin, Vladimir Ilyich 37
Lincoln, Abraham 33, **33**
Louis XIV, king of France 30, **30**, 31

M

Magna Carta 19
Marx, Karl 37
Mayas 24
Middle East 9, 12, 23, 41; *see also* Iran, Iraq, Muslim rulers, Persia
Moguls 26, **26**
  rulers 26, **26**, 27, 34
Mongols 23, 26
Montezuma II, Aztec ruler 24, **24**
Muslims 16, **16**, 17, **17**, 18, 20, 26, 39
  rulers 16, **16**, 17, **17**, 26, **26**, 27
Mussolini, Benito 38

N, O

Napoleon Bonaparte, ruler of France 30, 31, 35, 36, 42
Native American leaders 25, **25**, 32, 33
Nazi party 38, 39
Nefertiti, queen of Egypt **8**
Nero, Roman emperor 13
Netherlands, the 31, **31**

Octavian *see* Augustus, Roman emperor
Ottoman Empire 26, **26**, 37
  rulers 26, **26**

P

parliaments 19, **20**, 29, 36, 37, 38
Pericles, ruler of Athens 11
Perón, Eva and Juan 39, **39**
Persia 9, **9**, 11; *see also* Iran
Peter the Great, tsar of Russia 31
Poland 15, 40
popes 19, 21, 28, **28**, 29, **29**
Portugal 21, 35
presidents 33, **33**, 37, 38, **38**, 39, 40, 42
prime ministers 35, 36, 37, 38, **38**, 40
Protestants 29, **29**, 32
Prussia 30, 31, 37

Q, R

Qin Shi Huangdi, emperor of China 22, **22**, 23

M (Ramses column)

Ramses II, pharaoh of Egypt **8**
religion 9, **15**, 16, **16**, 23, 29, **31**, 32, 33; *see also* Christians, Islam, popes, Protestants, Catholics, Roman
republics 12, 31, 31
Richard the Lionheart, king of England **21**
Roman Empire 9, 12, **12**, 13, **13**, 14, 15, 18, **18**, 21, 42
  emperors 12, **12**, 13, **13**, 14, **18**, 42
Russia 15, 18, 21, 30, 31, **31**, 33, **37**; *see also* U.S.S.R.
  rulers of **18**, 31

S

Saxons 14, **14**, 15, **15**, 18
Scotland 13, 21, 29
Senate 12, **12**, 32
Serbs 26, 30
shoguns 23, **23**
slaves 11, **11**, 33, 34, 35
Slavs 15, **18**
Solomon, King 9, **27**
Spain 13, 17, 18, 24, **24**, 29, 30, 32, 34, **35**, 38
  rulers of 17, **20**, 38
Sparta **10**, 11
Stalin, Josef 38, 40
Suleyman the Magnificent 26, **26**
Syria 19, 26

T, U

Turkey 10, 17, 26, 37
  rulers of 26, **26**, 37; *see also* Ottoman Empire
Tutankhamen, pharaoh of Egypt **8**
tyrants 10, 11, **11**

United Nations 41
U.S. 32, **32**, 40, 42
  presidents of 33, **33**, 39, 40, 42, 43
U.S.S.R. 39, 40; *see also* Russia
  rulers of 37, **38**, 40

V, W

Victoria, queen 34, 36
Vikings 14, **14**, 15, **15**, 18, 20

warrior kings 7, **8**, 10, 14, 15
Washington, George 32, **33**, **33**